Through Hell And High Waters

One Woman's Incredible Journey To Faith

by
Almina Francis

authorHOUSE™

1663 Liberty Drive, Suite 200
Bloomington, Indiana 47403
(800) 839-8640
www.AuthorHouse.com

AuthorHouse™
1663 Liberty Drive, Suite 200
Bloomington, IN 47403
www.authorhouse.com
Phone: 1-800-839-8640

AuthorHouse™ UK Ltd.
500 Avebury Boulevard
Central Milton Keynes, MK9 2BE
www.authorhouse.co.uk
Phone: 08001974150

First published by AuthorHouse 11/1/2006

ISBN: 1-4184-8048-7 (e)
ISBN: 1-4184-8047-9 (sc)
ISBN: 1-4184-8046-0 (dj)

Library of Congress Control Number: 2005901407

Printed in the United States of America
Bloomington, Indiana

This book is printed on acid-free paper.

TABLE OF CONTENTS

I Owe It All To God

I would never feel complete if God wasn't given His rightful place in this book. Therefore, I place Him first and rely on His divine wisdom to find my place. If it is in serving, let me serve well; should it be in giving, let me give generously; and if it is in writing let me, in sharing my experience, bandage wounds that have been left exposed and revive dreams that have been shattered. If it is in showing appreciation, let me always remember to say Thank You to those who held my hands on the rocky pathway of life and refuse to let go even when I stumble and fall. If it is in cherishing memories, let me never forget the memories of a child whose death paved the way for my daughter's life. The death of one brings life to another. The death of a savior, hope for our world. Let this book serve as a reminder that it is only God who enables us to triumph over adversity. I owe it all to God, and I dedicate this book to He who brings hope to the hopeless and love to the loveless.

Think On These Words

Isaiah 42:16 (New International Version)

Along unfamiliar paths I will guide them; I will turn the darkness into light before them and will make the rough places smooth. These are the things I will do; I will not forsake them.

Jeremiah 29:11 (Amplified Version)

For I know the thoughts and plans that I have for you, says the Lord, thoughts and plans for welfare and peace and not for evil, to give you hope in your final outcome.

Isaiah 43:1-3 (Amplified Version)

Fear not, for I have redeemed you (ransomed you by paying a price instead of leaving you captives); I have called you by your name; you are Mine. When you pass through the waters, I will be with you, and through the rivers, they will not overwhelm you. When you walk through the fire, you will not be burned or scorched; nor will the flame kindle upon you. For I am the Lord your God, the holy One of Israel, your Savior.

Proverbs 3:5-6 (Amplified Version)

Lean on, trust in, and be confident in the Lord with all your heart and mind and do not rely on your own insight or understanding. In all your ways know, recognize and acknowledge Him, and he will direct and make straight and plain your paths.

Acknowledgments

It is with sincere appreciation and heartfelt gratitude that I wish to acknowledge my family and friends who have worked tirelessly in helping me to produce this book. Thank you for believing in me enough to support me through this very interesting transition in my life. My journey hasn't been easy, but because of your support, encouragement and commitment, I have been able to fulfill my dream as an author.

Many thanks to my mother and father, Estena and George Wittock for giving me a chance in life. Thanks to my beloved grandmother Almina James, who's now deceased; and also to my late uncle and his wife, James and Luna Burnett. Your input in my life has helped to make my dream come true.

My sincere appreciation to Merrick Francis, my wonderful and devoted husband, who stood by me every step of the way. Without your love and patience, this book would not have been possible. I also want to acknowledge Tamara Francis, my only daughter, who has inspired me to write this book. Thanks to Keiron McKenzie, my nephew, who has been very helpful and understanding, and to my two foster children, thanks for your love and patience. My niece, Sandra Edwards, has been my rock and I am extremely grateful for her support. Thank you Joan Williams and Craig Myers for your help and encouragement. It's very much appreciated.

Many thanks to all my other family members and friends: Kathleen Wittock, Sheila Ansine, the Burnett family, Eleen Minto, Yvonne Arthurs and the many others who have helped to make my dreams come true. Gillian Ramsey, your contribution to our lives is much appreciated. Thank you.

I also wish to acknowledge Dorrette Hanson for her help and support.

Thank you to Gillian James, who has worked tirelessly and faithfully over the past few months, helping to type my work. Those golden fingers have really worked wonders! Not only that, but she was on-hand to copy edit and proofread the manuscript. She's a multi-talented woman who is hard-working and has shown great determination in seeing this project through to the end. Your contribution has been invaluable, Gillian, and very much appreciated.

A big thanks to all the doctors and nurses at the Birmingham Children's Hospital who fought for my daughter's survival, and who were always available to answer our queries and concerns. Many thanks also to the doctors at The Handsworth Wood Medical Center for their kindness and encouragement. You have been consistent in supporting and caring for our daughter in one of the most traumatic times in our lives. Your commitment to our family has really made an impression on our lives and through your love, you have shown us that you value and respect your patients. We are privileged to be patients in your practice. Thank you very much.

My gratitude goes to my church family at Beacon Evangelical Church, for standing alongside me through the high and low times in my life. Many thanks to the members of the Monday Fellowship who continuously prayed for us and supported us in the difficult times.

To my pastors and their wives, Timothy and Edwina Turner, Eric and Sandra Jones, thank you for believing in me. Many thanks also to Charlene Larrier, Carol Tomlin and Michelle Lynch for your kindness. I could not complete these acknowledgments without saying a special Thank You to Sonia Lawrence and Selina Arthurs, who stood by Tamara all through her illness, offering comfort and reassurance. You have taught us the value of true friendship and commitment. Thank you.

Tamara and Mom

CHAPTER ONE
Destined for Trials

It all began on April 14, 1959 in Jamaica.

A sixth child was born to social injustice, poverty and deprivation. Yet again, another child, born in the slums of despair and inequality with no foreseeable future. A slave to her brutal environment and a shadow in the dark, lost and forgotten by a country that yields much, yet gives little to the rural areas. Despite this, the atmosphere in her small community was filled with optimism, laughter and fun, as people learnt to be content with the little they had. There was a strong bond of friendship and generosity amongst both the adults and children, as they supported each other during the difficult times. Who else is there to hold on to when poverty grips you with both hands and tries to strangle you of precious life? Nevertheless, there is still the whisper of a GOD who fights back and stands in your defense.

The island of Jamaica was beautiful with many hills, mountains and clear blue seas. Its luscious sceneries, tropical weather and warm and friendly inhabitants attracted people from many different countries, yet the economic situation meant that people from the rural areas would miss out on important opportunities. In a small community that was quiet and peaceful, this child became another victim of poverty and emotional trauma.

She faced a dismal future and such thoughts had ravaged her trust in a god that seemed so distant and passionless. There was nothing much to look forward to and little to believe in, yet the answers to her problems lay in the redemptive power of God. This she would later discover as she traveled life's treacherous pathway. Her family's only source of hope and comfort were Bible studies and daily prayers, which were introduced to her in a way that she dared not resist. Singing and praying were the norm, as both young and old sought refuge from the daily struggles of life, in the only One who creates life itself, GOD.

It was extremely difficult growing up in an environment that seemed so right, yet was so wrong. Everything appeared perfect as most people got on with their lives, doing their usual activities. Many mothers kept themselves busy in the kitchen whilst their husbands went to the fields to cultivate the crops. Youngsters got on with their busy schedules, sweeping the yard, fetching water from the tank or streams or collecting food from the fields. Despite this, people still found time to play games and have fun.

Life went on as normal. Hardly anyone complained about their predicament, there was no public protest against the oppression, and only SURVIVAL became the main focus of the day. Still, this little girl could not be contented. Each day as the sun set and the moon shone in the pitch darkness, she gazed at the sky and said to herself, "There has to be more to life than this."

Life seemed normal in the earlier years of her life. However, the grim reality of inferiority complex hit her like a brick in the face, as she stood in the company of her school friends one day, only to discover that she was the only one without shoes. Looking down at her feet made her want to disappear below the earth, as she noticed the dust from the sun-parched soil coated around her toes. This wasn't unusual in her community, yet the embarrassment sent shock waves down her spine and gave her a distaste for poverty and an overwhelming desire to resist it in every way, shape or form.

This young girl had a mother that loved, and a father who cared, yet their busy lives in the fields had distracted them from seeing the invisible tears, so frequently shed. Despite this, there was no one to blame, as this legacy had been passed down to her through the generations. This, however, didn't remedy the situation as she was left to tolerate illiteracy, arrogance and insensitivity, which rubbed shoulders together and created havoc in her life. Her other siblings were no better off than she was. Hard labor in the fields and the heat from the glaring sun made their lives unbearable. Poverty and hardship had ruined their hopes of an early escape from their torturous lifestyle, yet their trust in God was steadfast. This child's belief in God, however, was unsteady, as she needed some more answers for the misery that had become her constant companion.

Her self-esteem and confidence were sometimes low, and she fought hard to unravel the unfairness of life. How she wished there were no fields to go to and no tanks to draw water from. The fields had ruined her little hands and her thin and slender body had many scars from falling over. She was constantly being attacked by herbs and

3

shrubs, as she searched for a path through the thickets, to gather the produce from the fields. Her silent cries continued, "Where is God in all of this?" God seemed as far away as possible but she encouraged herself to pray.

Comfort was strangely found through prayer, but the answer to her existence was still a great mystery. Physical abuse was the norm in the small community. Yet no questions were asked, no voice of protest was heard, and everyone minded their own business. Still there was the voice of laughter from children playing on the street, and also from parents and grandparents who found great delight in telling fairy tales and ghost stories.

Amidst the hard life, pleasure and happiness visited this young girl every now and then, and she tried to make the best of the small blessings she had. Still she struggled to accept the environment in which she found herself. Her mind frequently raced to the following day, trying to figure out what the day had in store for her.

Was it going to be the arduous journey to the field called Jambos Pond, or would it be the dreaded trek to Omeally? It was hard to predict the events of the day as every trip to the fields left her numb with despair, yet the most daunting journey was the trip to Omeally. Its small and dangerous tracks seemed like miles uphill. These were surrounded with briers and thorns, which frequently obstructed her view and made it difficult to find her way around. Not only were there mosquitoes which feasted on her blood, leaving itchy red patches on her body, but also ants which viciously attacked her for accidentally stepping in their nest. Although the trip to Omeally was distressing, it could also be a pleasurable activity at times, as ripe fruits like mangoes, pineapples and guavas awaited her. To add to the excitement, her family would cook the produce from the land so that she would be fed and watered. Despite this, it was hard carrying the produce from the land to her home.

Soaked with sweat in the soaring sun was both unpleasant and uncomfortable, but her family told jokes and kept her spirits up. What was frightening was the mentally deranged man who strolled up and down her family's overcrowded field, looking for anything he could find. How could she and her family stay clear of this hefty-looking stranger who was sometimes very unpredictable? They were left to the mercy of God as they frequently hid to keep out of his way.

Living with her grandmother was like an interesting adventure. She was just minutes away from her own mother's house which sometimes created questions in other people's minds. She knew that her grandmother loved her dearly, and had chosen to take care of her from a young age, but she was not sure what age she went to live with her. She heard the story of how she got her name, and this fascinated her.

This was an illustration of sincere love from her grandmother. According to the story, when this young girl was born, her grandmother took one look at her and said to her mother, "Me we mine ye," meaning I will look after her. From that minute, everyone started calling her Miney, which became her pet name. Her grandmother went one step further, in naming this young girl after her to prove her love and commitment. Although she was grateful for her generosity, there were still pieces of the jigsaw missing.

Her grandmother loved her and did what she could to make her happy; yet, going to the field was not optional. This was not open for discussion; therefore the thought of going to the field filled her with great

5

anxiety and resentment. She hated the feeling of being trapped in poverty. She loved her grandmother but resented her strict code of discipline, which very often left no room for questions or explanations. As a child, she was not allowed to talk to boys or make regular visits to her friends, which left her feeling alienated at times.

This child found herself enslaved by her environment, chasing after the wind and being caught going round and round in the same vicious circle, just like her parents. She could not console herself as she thought of the fate that life had predetermined for her. She was not content living in an environment where she could not help herself, let alone the poor. That constantly troubled her mind. She felt like she should be helping to relieve the suffering of the poor and lift some of the strain from her own family; however, her present circumstance gave her no assurance of that happening.

The majority of people from her community were honest, respectable and hardworking. They had strong morals and values, which they tried to instill in the younger generation. Many senior citizens became her mentor as they taught respect and discipline. Their lifestyle showed great courage, perseverance and generosity and at times, there was a sense that everyone was looking out for each other. Some people seemed to have her interests at heart, and freely offered emotional support, advice and encouragement. In a strange way, she felt protected and shielded from the harsh realities of life.

Nevertheless, a few lacked self-control and discipline, and preyed on some of the young and vulnerable. Because of this, growing up was sometimes embarrassing, having to be subjected to the occasional stares and suggestive remarks from some of the men. This caused a rude awakening to her innocence.

At only 10 years old, this young girl managed to hold on to the morals and values she had been taught, despite not having much material possessions. Life for this child was far from being real. In her mind, life had become an impostor and a destructive force that broke her will and shattered her dreams. Yet, she yearned for a break from the heartache of watching her family and friends struggle. How she wished she could untie the ropes of poverty that had been strangling so many of her fellowmen. Where she got that inner passion from, she wasn't sure, but it resided in her young mind for a long time.

Maybe, one day God will deliver her from the grips of poverty and injustice. Maybe she will find an early escape from her overwhelming ordeal. Somehow, there has to be some respite from her difficulties. Who could possibly be this child who, despite the hardship, felt the love of a God who constantly cared for her? Who is this young girl who saw little hope in the distance, yet embraced courage and a determination to rise above the storms of life and triumph over adversity? Interestingly, this young girl was me.

CHAPTER TWO
A Bleak Future

Growing up in Mount Industry wasn't easy. This was a small district in the parish of St. Catherine, with approximately one thousand people living there. People's way of life was very simple and poverty-stricken, yet many managed to get on with their normal routine without grumbling. Although life was hard, there were still many happy and pleasant times.

In the summer, trees were crammed with fruits and vegetables and children eagerly embarked on their mission to gather their favorite fruits from the fields. The smell of ripe mangoes and apples and the budding flowers in the summer sun littered the atmosphere with a pleasant aroma. The air was filled with laughter as some of the youths spent their leisure time playing baseball or hide-and-seek games on the streets. The sound of dogs barking and the whistling of birds in the trees could be heard from a distance, but for the adults it was business as usual.

These were treasured and memorable experiences, which are difficult to forget, but the memories often fade when measured against the daily struggles for survival. Poverty was real and so was pain. For me poverty was a crime that should be fought both fiercely and vigorously, and should not be allowed to win.

In a district where men, women and children lived it was apparent that some people were prepared to accept their fate without a fight, while others were too tired to fight, as politicians seemed to close their ears to the desperate cries for help from our community. Our doom was therefore sealed to a life without electricity, no proper means of running water, no inside toilets and hardly any television. There were about three pipes to draw water from and two medium-size tanks to serve our community. The pipes were hardly in use as they were constantly being destroyed by some of the youngsters. Because of this, we had to resort to drawing water from the tank.

One of the tanks belonged to the local school, which we were prohibited from using, while the other one was built on the land of our local councillor. He was also a poor man, although a little better off than our family. There was no proper access to get to the tank and we had to travel through his cultivation, breaking down branches to clear the way. At times, we had to draw the water with a long rope and hoped that there was enough to serve all those in the queue. We were told on many occasions that some selfish delinquent had infested the tank with all manner of debris.

There were times when lizards and frogs accidentally plunged to their early deaths, leaving a nasty smell in the water. Mosquitoes and flies freely made their entry into the tank at any given opportunity, leaving us with no option but to resort to the small spring through our parents' cultivation. The journey was both dangerous and difficult, as it had overgrown bushes and very small tracks that could only hold one person at a time. One bad move could be fatal as you waded precariously through the brambles to make your way home. There was also the risk of meeting the mentally disturbed man who frequently prowled around that area. The thought of bumping into him with his sharp knife or machete sent spasms of anxiety and fear through our bodies. Such hardship was distressing.

Needless to say, life was hard and for me, unbearable. At the age of about ten God had planted a massive vision in my mind to help the poor, which seemed absolutely impossible to fulfill in a community where degradation reigned. Most people's main source of income was agriculture—growing bananas, yams, ackees, plantains, callaloo and many other vegetables, and taking them to the market on a truck that was packed like sardines.

People and their produce mixed together on the same truck. For many, standing up between their homegrown products, while holding on to the truck with one hand and traveling approximately twenty-two miles to Kingston, was a normal way of life. Battered and bruised, they went to Princess Street to sell their produce. This was a filthy downtown market surrounded by dirty water and packed with rubbish. Looters and thieves often prowled on nearby streets.

Although the journey was long and laborious, it was interesting and full of excitement, as I had the opportunity of passing through the nicer areas of Kingston. As the truck roared through the crowded streets, I caught faint glimpses of the suburban lifestyle, which further enticed me to continue to pursue a better way of life. Rows of attractively designed houses lined the streets with breathtakingly beautiful views whilst expensive cars filled the driveways.

Kingston was a picturesque city with exquisite buildings and magnificent scenery. Beautiful pine trees and lovely gardens with flowers budding in the summer sun, added a touch of elegance and sophistication to the urban lifestyle. Some people walked briskly with a sense of pride and achievement, while others bore the mark of poverty and destitution. As the truck grated along the stony roads, it was incredible to see the wide gap between the rich and the poor. The momentary pleasure of passing through, what could be described as paradise, faded into the distance as I approached the uninviting squalor of downtown Kingston.

Shacks and derelict buildings littered the overcrowded streets as both young and old scurried about to sell their belongings, while others sprawled on the sidewalk yelling for shoppers to buy their produce. The divide between the rich and poor was startling and I was left baffled as I tried to make sense of what I had just seen. It didn't take long before we arrived at our destination, and for us it was business as usual.

As a youngster, it was difficult for me to help my mother sell nutmegs and other produce from the land. Having to carry around the nutmegs and trying to sell them on the odd occasion was no fun. It was embarrassing to hear children shout "A dollar for a dozen nutmegs, come and buy."

Mother was unable to give us a better life, although she did the best she could with the limited resources she had. She was a kind and fairly intelligent woman who enjoyed public speaking and having Bible studies with her children. She worked very hard on the land to provide for us, yet still found time to help other members of the community. Father was placid and easygoing and had hardly attended school. There was a twenty-one year age gap between them, but they had a good relationship.

Being a family of nine made it extremely difficult for any of us to survive or even live with the dignity that we deserved. We spent most of our early years walking barefoot on the hot ground, bucking our toes on stones and with prickles or broken glass in our feet, which was the painful chore of our grandma to extract. This was both terrifying and painful and our screams could sometimes be heard from a distance.

Grandma was fairly strong when my brother and I lived with her. She lived in a small house made of concrete and board with four medium sized bedrooms. My uncle's wife and four children also lived there and she shared the responsibility of raising us. My uncle's wife was a jovial and caring woman who worked very hard at home looking after the family. Although her life was far from easy, she still found time to encourage and support us in whatever way she could. There was a mixture of pleasure, laughter and sometimes animosity but over the years, we learnt the true value of sharing and giving. Obviously, space was a problem as there were not enough rooms to go around, so my brother and I slept in the same bed with grandma— my brother at the top while grandma and I slept at the bottom.

There was no space for privacy and I felt trapped at times, as reading or doing any type of homework was sometimes impossible.

As children, we were at times stubborn and disobedient, and often we would pay the price. Our normal routine was to collect water, sweep the yard, polish and shine the floor and then the other duties would follow. One morning, grandma sent us to the pipe to collect water and told us to hurry back as quickly as possible. On arriving at the pipe, there were many other children waiting to draw water, and we had to wait our turn.

While waiting, a few of us decided to play racing on the street. As we ran up and down the street, a strange sensation hit the bottom of my right foot that sent spasms of discomfort through my body. It wasn't painful at first, so I continued running until the race was finished. I sat on the side of the road to check my foot, only to discover a large piece of green glass stuck all the way in my heel.

With blood pouring from my foot and a tear-stained face, I waited patiently for my turn to collect the water. After filling my large bucket, I carefully put it on my head and hopped my way home in excruciating pain, worrying what my grandma was going to say. As soon as she saw my face and heard my quiet whimpering, she realized that something was wrong, and hurried to help me lift the bucket from my head. As the bucket reached the ground, I began to scream uncontrollably. "My foot, my foot," I moaned. "Am I going to die?" The pain was too much for me to explain any further, so I pointed to my foot in an attempt to show grandma my injury.

Grandma took one look at my foot and nearly fell back. There was a thick piece of glass about two inches long, stuck into my heel. Blood flowed freely as I wrestled with the intense pain and discomfort. I could hardly control my screams, as the pain seemed to intensify. I wailed unashamedly and some of my neighbors came to enquire what was happening. After a brief explanation, grandma got to work straightaway. Laying me on my back, she washed my foot, pouring a small drop of bay rum in the wound. She then used a needle to try to remove the glass. After many unsuccessful attempts, she decided to try her own home remedy.

13

She then grated a green banana and the skin, and added kerosene oil to it. After heating the mixture in a small tin, she put it on a piece of cloth and tied it under my heel. This was intended to slowly draw out the broken glass. Over the next few days I was stuck at home in unbearable pain waiting for the healing process to take place. It was a very unpleasant experience and I struggled to make use of my time, although I was glad not to be at school, as the teachers usually made our lives hell.

In approximately one week, the glass came out by itself, as a result of grandma's home remedy, and the pain gradually subsided. By the following week, I was once again back to my normal routine and had returned to school. Visiting a doctor was a rare occasion, except in life or death situations, or if a home remedy failed to work.

My brother and I were now settled with grandmother. She was well loved by the community because of her warmth and generosity. Although I loved my grandmother very much, there were still a few unanswered questions on my mind. I was still not sure how old I was when I went to live with her. All I could recall was being there and wishing I had a closer relationship with my parents. I didn't envy my brothers and sisters, as life was extremely hard for them too. All I wanted were some answers. For some reason it was important for me to know.

My grandmother lived close to mother, but I preferred to live with her, as mother spent most of her time in the fields, and there was hardly any time to see friends, or do other activities. Our complete energy was taken up with working for our survival, as father was always sick. Both his feet were always swollen and looked disfigured. He was never able to walk more than a few yards, and had to use a donkey to take him from one place to the other. The donkey was fun to have around, but it added more responsibilities to our already busy schedule.

Our added chore was to clean its mess when it was tied in front of our house, and find grass for its feed. Once we were out of our parents' sight we took our turns to practice riding our donkey, sometimes two of us at once. Many attempts to ride him often left us battered and bruised, as he would deliberately race down the stony roads with us hanging on for dear life and screaming at the top of our voices. The donkey often refused to stop until we were thrown in the branches of some small trees or on the stony roads. Our adventures always ended up in tears leaving us to nurse our cuts and bruises. Although it was a lovely donkey, it could be very vicious at times, kicking us without warning, sometimes in the chest, head and legs. Life was cruel to us and so was our father's donkey!

My uncle, who was living in England, arrived home after ten years, and our relationship was great. It was lovely to have another father figure I could look up to. I loved my uncle. Although he was very strict with his own children, we got along well. I was close to his children and we had many fun times together. My uncle's daughter, Gillian, and I were particularly close and we had great ideas and plans of how to escape poverty, although we were not sure how these would materialize. Our time would often be spent in discussion, making plans for the future, going to the fields and doing house chores. These were good and memorable times that I cherish even to this day, but that didn't alter my disgust for poverty and the social degradation that stared us in the face on a daily basis.

Life was monotonous and full of confusion, and at times I felt forgotten by the world and also by this caring GOD that our parents spoke about. If He really cared why was I feeling so lost and dejected? There was stability, insofar as I had a roof over my head, but I was plagued by this overwhelming desire to make some sense of my plight.

Discipline via physical punishment was the normal way of life in my grandma's house. Any misunderstanding or slight disagreement greeted us with severe beatings with small branches from the rose tree in front of our house. Real conversations between our parents and us were rare, and laughter and joy had mysteriously disappeared from their faces. Such was the pressure of life and the brutality of poverty that the once beautiful faces of our parents now carried the marks of overwhelming fatigue and heartache. There was no rest for the weary, no time to relax and no time for self-pity. It was an ongoing struggle for survival.

I had very close relationships with my sisters and we met regularly to discuss our plight. My heart broke as I watched their struggles and the intense pressure that life had so ruthlessly shoved in their path. They were forced to grow up and assume the responsibilities of adults. Their life revolved around wading through thorns and briers to search for brambles for the fire, and regularly going to the fields to dig yams, chop coconuts, cut canes and then carry home their produce through the scorching sun. Ants and ticks bites, scratches and bruises made their lives hell. How I wished that I were in a position to help alleviate some of the insurmountable pain that they faced on a daily basis. Their lives were by far worse than mine, as grandma would, at times, shield me from the arduous journeys to the field; but for my sisters, this was their way of life. There was absolutely no way of escape.

Although I lived with my grandmother, mother would often come to collect me to take me to the field, where we helped to get the produce ready for sale at the market. This involved helping to dig the produce and carry it through the bushes in the broiling sun. By the time we reached our destinations we were just about ready for bed. Exhaustion and tiredness made our sleep very miserable. We were too tired to sleep and too tired to stay awake. It was an absolute nightmare.

I hated the field, I hated poverty, and sometimes I hated LIFE itself. Oftentimes, I wished that my life were different. For me it was unbearable as I had visions of a better life. I am not sure if my brothers and sisters felt the same way, but I was certain that they were living the same nightmare as me.

CHAPTER THREE
My Encounter with Christ

My mother, father and grandmother were all God-fearing people. We were taught to pray and read the Bible and were sent to Sunday School every week, come rain or shine. We were hardly allowed to go to parties or any other social events except church-related ones. Our Christmas and Easter were spent studying the Bible and praying. There was hardly any excitement in our lives. Church was very boring at times and I hated going there. The ministers often used words that were difficult to understand. It really did not appeal to me and, every opportunity I got, I would hide my shoes hoping that I didn't have to attend the service. However, nothing would deter my grandmother from sending us to church, even if it meant going without shoes!

On one occasion, my sister and I devised a plot for us not to go to church. We went a few chains away from home, rubbed dirt on our dresses, elbows and knees, and went back home crying at the top of our voices. When our mother came to inquire we told her that we fell and hurt ourselves. Thinking that she would sympathize with us was a great misjudgment on our part! Instead, she chased us down the rocky hill, shouting, "Even if your foot is broken, you are going to church." We ran as fast as we could to escape being caught and beaten viciously for our deception.

My sister and I went to church that Sunday feeling very embarrassed and humiliated. There was dirt still on our clothes, elbows and knees, as we never had time to wash it off. We paid a dear price for lying!

My older sister and I had a few church dresses that my mother made. These were worn on alternate Sundays. We had one pair of shoes, which were only worn to church or on special occasions. We had to go everywhere else barefooted. School was an ordeal, as our teachers were sometimes very cruel and would beat us mercilessly for being late and for getting any of our schoolwork wrong. There was no escape from brutality as corporal punishment was the norm in our society.

Many times, we resented the idea of going to school as we were beaten regularly. Any form of disability or visual impairment weren't taken into consideration, and some children suffered because of this. As parents struggled to make ends meet, severe medical conditions were sometimes missed, leaving their children vulnerable and open to abuse. Greater still was the humiliation of going to school without shoes. Those feelings were too deep to be put into words, yet we had to suffer the embarrassment day after day, hoping that soon God would bring an end to our misery.

Our school was approximately one mile from home, but there were times when we were late, because of our busy schedule. After running all the way to school, we would reach assembly almost out of breath. Some of the teachers were not only immature but also deeply insensitive towards our feelings, and made remarks concerning our appearance. This was embarrassing for us, especially when they talked about children coming to school with their "10 Testament" on the ground (meaning barefooted). Being ridiculed for something that was beyond our control was not fair.

There were two schools in our district, which we called Top and Bottom Schools. The Top School was in the same vicinity as the Anglican Church, and the Bottom School was on the same site as the Baptist church. There were other churches in the small district of Mount Industry, but we sometimes visited The Church of God of Prophecy and Full Gospel House of Prayer. They were completely different from the Baptist church that we attended. People were lively; they played guitar and worshipped God.

The things that were happening in those churches captivated us. We wanted to learn more, so we attended our church in the mornings and the Church of God churches in the evenings. Our appetite for learning developed as our visits became more frequent. I loved going to the Prophecy Church, as there was one woman who really got the people's attention.

She was tall and slender and was always dancing. She made funny gestures with her hands, rocked her head from side to side, twisted her tiny frame and shouted at the top of her voice, "Hallelujah" until the whole place seemed to shake. She was vibrant and it was amazing to see her praising God all the time. I would always 'end up in stitches' as I watched her. For some reason I couldn't control my laughter and ended pressing my hands against my mouth to try and control myself. She was an amazing woman, and the first one I ever saw operating in the gifts of the Spirit. Somehow, I was taken aback by this woman and couldn't wait to visit the church in order to watch her and have some fun.

There were also the usual prophecies in the church, and these fascinated me. I became more and more interested in the gifts of the Spirit, so we continued visiting, in order to develop our understanding of the scriptures and to try and make sense of what was taking place.

I was not yet a Christian, but I had thought about it many times. One Sunday, a group of us visited the Church of God of Prophecy in Freedom (a tiny district on the edge of Mount Industry), as there was a crusade. I was only about thirteen years old at the time, and my sole purpose was to watch the woman who always "jerked in the Spirit" or engaged in her routine performance. I called her "Sister Jerker."

When I got to the church, it was packed to capacity, as other churches were invited to this special occasion. I sat at the back of the church. The meeting began and it was very lively; children were dancing and worshiping God and the whole atmosphere was electrifying. I caught a glimpse of Sister Jerker and I could not help but laugh as she spun around, wiggled and twisted her body. One could not help but notice this woman of about sixty years old, so meticulously dressed and yet so enthusiastic and vibrant about her faith.

After the worship, there were testimonies and exhortations. It was amazing to see children as young as seven and eight testifying and sharing about the goodness of God. For me it was 'mind blowing.' The minister was then called to preach. He was a young man in his early thirties who spoke enthusiastically about the love of God. We grew up knowing his family who struggled to make ends meet. He lived in a small house with his wife and children, who were all involved in church life.

Questions started entering my mind. "How can a God that loves so much allow his servant to face such poverty?" "How can this young man speak so enthusiastically about God when his very basic needs haven't

21

even been met?" This created unease within me and a passion for something better.

All I wanted was to have the basic necessities of life and see my parents comfortable, with a place I could call home, not somewhere I was ashamed of, or embarrassed to show my friends. I could not control my thoughts as they went all over the place, and for some reason, I didn't want to. I desperately needed to fit the pieces of the puzzle together. Nothing seemed to be making sense.

My mind went back to the earlier times when I visited my friend's home in Cassava River. She was so proud of where she lived that she gave us a tour of her house. They had a refrigerator, television, cooker and indoor toilet, and I was taken aback by their level of prosperity. Her relationship with her parents was extremely good, and they chatted and played together like real friends. How I wished I had a few of the luxuries they had. After seeing her house, how was I going to return the invitation? I was determined that there was no way my friend was coming to visit us.

All of a sudden, I was aware of my surroundings again. I was in church. The minister was talking about the love of God and I was curious about Him. For some unknown reason I struggled with the idea of God versus poverty. I just couldn't bring the two together. Out of the corner of my eye, I could see Sister Jerker about to let loose in the Spirit, and I began to smile again. The service was extremely good and I was really enjoying it, except for moments when I was interrupted by these overwhelming thoughts.

As I made an effort to listen to the minister, what seemed like a ton of bricks hit me. His next words were, "Jesus loves you just as you are." I had heard those words many times before, but for some reason today; it was pulling at my heartstring. *Jesus loves me just as I am!* I said to myself. Me, the one whom everyone teased about being ugly. I pondered about those words very carefully because, just a few days ago, I had been told by one of my cousins that I was the ugliest of my mother's nine children, and that statement really rocked my world. With an already low self-esteem and my shoddy appearance, I could not help but creep into a corner and hope to die. Tears streamed down my face as I went to the cracked, fuzzy mirror in the bedroom to have another look at myself. Sadly, I came out believing the lie my cousin told me. I was really ugly.

It was important for me to hear even the very mention of the word *love,* because occasionally I felt unloved and alone with my thoughts. The echoes of people's crude comments were deafening me. I could hear the horrible words, the nicknames and the torturous remarks that trampled my self-esteem to nothing.

The incident at school a week earlier was still fresh in my mind and I was again reliving those terrible nightmares. About twenty of us as classmates were shoved into a merciless and pitiful contest, where one person volunteered herself as the judge. She decided to choose the prettiest, right down to the ugliest person in the class.

How could she have such a contest when she looked so worn and battered by life's cruel and hostile hands? Her face was hard and rigid and her hands and arms were so muscular, it appeared as if a basketball had lost its way there. Her two calves and large disfigured stomach showed signs of malnutrition. Yet, here she was, living under the shambles of deceit and self-hatred, trying to belittle someone in order to feel good about herself. I held my breath as she reached fifteen. Still there was no mention of my name. Sixteen, seventeen, eighteen, nineteen. Here I was again, number twenty, the ugliest person in the group.

Life again had kicked me in the face and left me seriously wounded. I was once again dragged and tossed about by life's vicious hands. Love had impolitely walked out of my life and left me battered and bruised. How I longed for LOVE to reappear, throw its arms around me and reassure me that it was going to be all right.

The words of that young minister echoed repeatedly in my mind. JESUS LOVES YOU JUST AS YOU ARE. And he continued, "All you have to do is receive His LOVE through forgiveness of sins." In a minute, my life flashed in front of me and I wanted this love so badly. I wanted it in any way, shape or form. I just wanted LOVE. My quest for love had become a matter of urgency, and I bowed my head and asked the greatest love of all to come into my life.

As soon as I said those words, an overwhelming presence invaded my space, and I began to speak in a strange language. I felt as if I was being lifted out of my seat and carried to the altar. I stayed at the altar, for what seemed a long time, enjoying this supernatural experience, and for the first time, feeling a love that I had never known before. I could not stop thanking God, my lips felt light and there was a strange sense of PEACE around me that was too difficult for words to explain. LOVE lifted me that Sunday night.

CHAPTER FOUR
A New Experience

The experience left me on a high for many months, but strangely enough, it did not get rid of the problems. I was the same little thirteen-year-old girl with the same problems, living in the same poverty-stricken environment, but with a newfound friend. I felt great comfort from the knowledge that Jesus loves me and accepts me just as I am. The thoughts of my classroom horror still haunted me. I hated my cousin for saying I was ugly, but I had a friend with whom I could share those feelings.

I had many things to talk to God about, many questions to ask and many conflicts to resolve, so I spent many hours talking with Him. From the depths of my despair, I began to feel a glimmer of hope. The Bible had become a new acquaintance and, bit-by-bit, I began to understand that God had big plans for my life. It still didn't change how I felt about POVERTY. I was as determined as ever not to let my environment enslave me, but to fight my way through the thorns of deprivation and injustice. How I was going to do that I wasn't sure but, with God on my side, I knew I would escape my horrendous nightmare.

There was no doubt that my life was beginning to take a new shape. With all that was going on around me, I became enthusiastic about God and the need to go to church became overwhelming. I prayed frequently even though I had many unanswered questions. My sisters and I started attending the Youth Club, which was packed with interesting activities. This was excellent as it gave us an opportunity to study and develop our talents.

Life was like a roller coaster as I was still trying to come to terms with my new experience. However, there was clear evidence of change in the way I viewed things. My mind was slowly becoming clearer and instead of having the usual nightmares in my sleep, I was now beginning to have pleasant recurring dreams, which were sometimes very therapeutic. In my dream, I always had a car with two suitcases neatly packed inside. After viewing my surroundings that had enslaved me for so many years, I finally sped away, saying, "I refuse to let you haunt me anymore, I am leaving in search of my destiny."

When I awoke, the feeling of emancipation filled me with joy and lifted my spirit to a higher place. Hope cradled me in that hour and peace waved at me. I felt like I was climbing out of the abyss of despair into the shelters of a new horizon. The feeling of being wrapped in woolly blankets covered with the essence of hope was a liberating one. Although the experience was often short-lived, I clenched on to its memory as long as I could. Other dreams of people and events invaded my sleep and for some strange reason, they were making sense.

Could it be that God was trying to tell me something? Was it His way of telling me that He was there with me? I wasn't sure, but it was an interesting experience. All I knew was that I was on a journey with valleys and mountain tops experiences, and at any given time I could be somewhere between the two. At that moment I was immersed in the small pleasures I got from my dreams and I wasn't going to let go of it lightly. Interestingly, those moments did pass swiftly and became distant memories that faded with the wind.

This may sound like a strange scenario for people who cannot relate to my life, but for me it was like the firm arm of hope embracing me in the midst of despair. Any thread of hope was a small step towards a new horizon. Exchanging the weight of poverty for a momentary delight was worth more than wallowing in self-pity. It is incredible how soon the gruesome reality of life reappear tapping me on my shoulder and waking me up to my situation. Despite all the events in my life I had a reason to carry on. Something was making me a little more courageous.

It was apparent that something extraordinary was happening to me. At church, I had a new experience; I was now beginning to engage in Bible studies and prayer. My attitude to life was slowly changing and there were small changes in my behavior. I was happier because there was a slight glimmer of hope of a brighter future.

As young people, we were active in the life of the church, and God's Spirit was manifested in a powerful way. Service was extremely vibrant and the attendance grew rapidly.

CHAPTER FIVE
The Ultimate Betrayal

The day scheduled for my baptism was Good Friday. There were other young people who were to be baptized on the same day, and we were all looking forward to it. This was a time of thanksgiving and deep reflections about life. There was a spirit of anticipation in the church as our young people prepared for their new experience.

I was on a spiritual high. I felt overwhelmed by God's presence as I spent many days in prayer. All I wanted to do was to thank God for loving me, even when I found it hard to love myself. My conversion was an experience that words couldn't describe. It felt like someone had reached down into my grave and pulled me out, carefully dusting all the dirt from my body. The dirt that buried me in self-hatred, oppression and degradation, was slowly being cleared away and, in the distance, I could now see a faint glimmer of hope. That was enough to keep me ticking on.

The week before my baptism my older cousins decided to go to the shop to do our usual shopping. Although it was a lovely Saturday, for some reason I wasn't in the mood for socializing and would have rather spent the time at home. However, with gentle persuasion from my cousins, I decided to go with them. Since it was early evening and we had a small shopping list, there was no harm in having a walk down to the Square. Things were difficult and we could only afford a few items, which included cooking oil, hard dough bread, sugar, flour, salt and rice. Therefore, we were expected to be back home soon.

Our chicken had already been caught and tied to the kitchen post, ready for our Sunday meal. Part of our regular routine was to collect dry wood from the field to cook the food. This was our way of life and, although we detested it, there was no other choice available to us.

That same evening my three cousins and I went to the shop. The sky was hardly lit, as there were no electric lights in our district, yet we strolled down the steep road chatting and laughing. It was a lovely evening as we watched people mingling with each other and the occasional vehicle passing by.

On reaching the shop, I decided not to go inside, as I wasn't in the talking mood. I was also conscious about my appearance and the fact that I had no shoes on. It was a Saturday evening and most people came out properly dressed, shoes and all, and here I was feeling ashamed, trying to hide my dusty feet. People could be insensitive at times and their remarks about your appearance were off-putting. With those thoughts in mind, I stayed outside and told my cousins I would wait for them there.

Although I was enjoying my new Christian experience, I still felt embarrassed about my appearance. I felt life had treated me unfairly as all my cousins had shoes on and I was the only one without. How I wished for a little of the luxuries that others had!

Even though life was difficult, God was doing a remarkable work in my life. I still had a hard time with the concept of God versus poverty and, at times, I struggled to make sense of my life. Even with my new-found friend, I had moments when I felt like giving up. On this occasion, overwhelming sadness visited me and drove me down the road of despair. Embarrassment had somehow gotten the better of me and left me with a feeling of despondency.

I stood outside the shop with mixed emotions. I was fascinated by the power of God, yet feeling ashamed of how I looked. Deep down I knew that God loved me despite my appearance, but the thought of being ugly still haunted me every now and then. It was difficult to reconcile the two trains of thought, and I found myself on an emotional roller coaster.

The struggle for survival was a harsh reality that I could not avoid. I would rather escape, but I had no choice but to carry on. These thoughts plagued my mind as I waited for my cousins.

It was a very busy Saturday evening. Many people were walking around, while others were busy doing their shopping. Some people stood in the dimly lit street enjoying the company of their friends, others "limed" by the side of the road, eating freshly baked bread and having a drink. I felt safe as I could see my cousins from where I stood, and this was a familiar place to me.

I stood on the top of a flight of stairs that led to a house below. Lost in my own world, I became aware of a voice. It was the familiar voice of a teacher from the local school. I looked ahead and saw him coming up the stairs. There was no sense of alarm or panic as this was a well-respected member of our community. With a smile on his face, this strapping, hairy-faced man came and stood beside me. "Let's go downstairs," he said. "No," I replied. He said, "Come on," and before I could say another word, he pulled me down the stairs as fast as he could. No amount of pleading and begging would make him change his mind. As the door of the house slammed behind me, I immediately knew I was in trouble. All the excuses I made failed to impress him as he was determined to satisfy his mood.

Life stood still for a while as I tried to make sense of what was taking place. All the misery I had been through in my short life flooded my memory. I was scared, nervous and confused. What about my baptism? Where is the God that promised to look after me? I couldn't understand what was happening and why it was happening to me. What was I going to tell my cousins? Life had again kicked me in the face and had left me dazed and confused.

Before I knew it, this beast of a man was on top of me and I was begging him to let me go. All of a sudden, a surge of anger raced through my body, and I wrestled with this creature with every ounce of energy I had. How dare this man try to violate my body without respecting my wishes! I fought, struggled and pleaded but nothing worked. Unfortunately, my strength ran out. I wanted to scream but the humiliation would be too great for me. How would I be able to live this down in such a small district where everyone knew each other?

Someone must have seen what happened because a few minutes later, there was a knock on the front door. The person was calling his name. "I want to talk to you," the voice on the other side of the door said. "I'm coming," he said, but that didn't deter him. Instead, he finished his business before opening the door and letting me out in the pitch darkness.

What was I supposed to do? It was dark and I was afraid of the ghosts that my grandmother talked about. I found it difficult to go home on my own as I felt physically sick. What was I going to tell them? How would I explain my disappearance to my cousins? Shaken and confused, I made my way around the house, which stood on the edge of a precipice, to avoid being noticed. I held on to anything I could find, only too aware that one wrong move could cost me my life. The night was dark and frighteningly quiet and there was hardly any sound coming from the streets as most people had gone home. I was petrified. I stepped gingerly and my movements were cautious and slow, as I struggled my way out of the gully using both hands and feet. After what seemed like hours, I finally made it back to the main road. My face was soaked with tears as the grim reality of what happened dawned on me. I peered around in the dark trying to look for my cousins, but there was no sign of them. They had all gone home. It was all too much for me to take in, so I sobbed uncontrollably.

Sex was a taboo subject; it wasn't discussed or talked about by anyone in our community. To entertain any discussion about it was unheard of. All I could remember hearing from my grandmother was, "Be careful of men because they are no good." That was the closest we had ever come to hearing about the "birds and the bees."

This person did something bad to me but I didn't have a name for it. I had never heard of RAPE before. I was far too innocent and naïve. What about my baptism? I felt useless and dirty. Would God ever forgive me for committing this act of sin? Why was I being punished? What was happening in my life?

All sorts of questions raced through my mind as I struggled to come to terms with what had happened. Could it be that God was punishing me for my sins? Once again I felt like I was skidding down a slippery slope and there was no one to catch me. The grief was too much for me, and in my mind's eye, I could see myself lying in a precipice with all my hopes and dreams dashed to pieces. Could God not have heard the noise of the torture of the innocent? Who is there to protect us from such violation and evil that continue to pursue us? Was I the only one, or were there countless others whose voices had been drowned by the constant struggle for survival? God forbid that such perverts should go unnoticed, and carry out more vicious acts on an unsuspecting child.

I must have cried out to God because, out of nowhere, a familiar face appeared. He inquired what I was doing out so late on my own. I cannot remember what I told him, but he took me part of the way home. At the bottom of the hill I could hear my grandmother cursing. As we got closer, her voice grew louder and louder, and I could hear some of the words she was saying. "Worthless gal"(worthless girl); "Man eena dem head"(only thinking about men); "She need lick drop in her backside"(she needs a beating). All those remarks were referring to me. I did not know where to put my face as we were bombarded with my grandmother's torturous remarks. After my humiliating experience, he encouraged me to go home and wished me all the best. I stood in silence for a few minutes, wishing that I could disappear and never be seen again.

With every energy I had, I mustered up the courage and walked home. The light from the house was dim, as everyone was already in bed.

CHAPTER SIX
The Big Interrogation

My grandmother greeted me with great hostility and intense anger. "Where are you coming from?" I tried to make up some excuse but the quarrelling and cursing became so fierce, it was worse than being hit. I actually thought my grandmother would hurt me badly, as she was so angry.

The night passed with me being very confused, sobbing uncontrollably, as I felt desperate and alone. There was no one to share my problems with and no shoulder to cry on. How I wished there was someone to tell me everything was going to be all right. I was very angry at what my attacker did to me, but I was also upset not being able to share it with anyone.

My brother and I were still sharing the room with my grandmother. We were sleeping in the same bed, with my brother at the top and me and my grandmother at the bottom. There was nowhere even to be alone with my thoughts. I desperately wanted to scream or thump the wall, but was unable to do so, as every room in the house was occupied. There was no outlet for my frustration, so I sobbed quietly beside my grandmother, turning my back to her, trying not to make any noise.

I didn't sleep the whole night because of sheer confusion. On Sunday morning, my cousins took turns questioning me. "Where were you?" "Did something happen to you?" "Where did you go?" We kept looking for you. It's as if you had disappeared off the face of the earth." I kept quiet—something had happened to me but I didn't have a name for it. Although we were close, we didn't talk about such issues. I wasn't going to begin now.

My heart was bursting with pain but my lips were sealed. How was I going to tell someone what happened to me, when I wasn't sure what it was called? Maybe if I had learned the word "RAPE", I would probably have said it and ran a mile, but there was no way to explain it without going into details, and I never had the courage anyway.

I was determined not to let anyone into my haunted world, because my experience was far too painful for words. The constant interrogation was now tearing me apart and I felt bombarded by the questions that were thrown in my direction. For some reason my life felt strange. The experience of being alone was real to me, and for a while, it was difficult to shake the feeling. It was hard for me to understand the intense feeling of loneliness, even though I was surrounded by so many people.

At times, I was being misunderstood as I tried to act as normal as possible. Acting tough or talking back to my grandmother didn't help. It only got me into more trouble. I was at a loss as to how to act or behave. Should I ignore the people I meet on the street, or should I act as if I just didn't care? After careful consideration, I decided to try the latter.

With great effort I tried to put on a brave face, with all the noise of last night still ringing in my ears. It was as if a hundred bullets had gone off and the sound was still blasting all around me. I could not escape the rumbling voice of torment that seemed to stalk me everywhere I went. Aiming to confront my pain and frustrations, I set to work scrubbing everything in my path. I cleaned the house thoroughly, swept the yard and then went to the spring to draw numerous buckets of water. For some unknown reason it was important for me to be involved in some type of activity. Being inactive was slowly pushing me over the edge, so I engaged myself with any type of work I could put my hands to. All of a sudden, it became a matter of urgency for me to return to the small spring, on my own, to have a bath. I could not control the sudden urge and I hurriedly made my way there.

At the edge of the small spring, I watched the water drifting slowly downstream, carrying with it all the soggy leaves and broken debris. Occasionally, I caught a glimpse of lizards curling up under the branches of the banana trees above, and frogs jumping from place to place with not a care in the world. As I stood there motionless, lost in my own world, I felt a strange sense of calm. I wished that the stream would take my pain away as it washed the debris downstream so I would never face it again. I also watched the cloud drifting over the morning sky and marveled at the wonders of creation, as rays of sunlight seemed to perch on my forehead.

It was an incredible feeling as the tiny rays of sunlight appeared like the welcomed presence of a friend. It was as if someone had visited me and was showing me light in the midst of the darkness. In my loneliness, I began to talk to it as if it were a person. Have you come to visit me, oh sunlight? Have you seen the pain and misery that has befallen me? Do you always hide behind the dark clouds or have you come to embrace me with your light? For a while the light lingered on my forehead, applying heat that seemed to massage my head, then slowly disappeared behind the horizon.

It was a therapeutic experience, as every movement of nature seemed to have some significance. As the breeze rumbled through the trees and the branches swayed to and fro, it appeared as if they were waving at me and saying, "It's going to be all right." I frantically waved back, with a smile on my face as if to say, yes, I know things will eventually get better. I desperately needed someone to console me and nature was doing a good job. Was it God who had stopped by to reassure me of His presence or was it my imagination playing tricks with me? I wasn't sure but somehow I chose to believe the former, because the momentary peace I had was beyond human understanding. I wished the moment wouldn't pass, but reality soon stepped in and the events of yesterday once again flooded my thoughts.

After what seemed like several minutes, I finally had my bath. I scrubbed my body for more than ten minutes, hoping that the pain would go away. Unfortunately, it never did. Numbed by the enormity of my ordeal, I tearfully and reluctantly made my way home. I wished that I could have spent more time standing under the shadows of the rock, watching the waters go by and listening to the voice of the birds and the rustling of the leaves.

Minutes later I was home. Not knowing what to expect, I sat on the steps outside our house in a thoughtful mood. I was approached by my uncle's wife who asked me to go to the shop. I was glad to get away as this gave me another opportunity to be on my own. My nightmare soon returned to haunt me, as I was again being questioned about my ordeal. This time, it was not by my family, but an adult in my community, who proceeded to reprimand me about my careless lifestyle. Now was the time to act as if I did not care, so I stared this fifty-year-old woman in the eyes, with a slight grin on my face, and said nothing. This was one time I felt like being disrespectful to an adult, but I couldn't! I wasn't raised that way.

Putting on a brave face, I walked away, forcing back the tears. Once out of her sight, I allowed my tears to flow freely. Fierce anger and hostility gripped my body. I could not hold back my emotions as I clenched my small fists in frustration and rage, waiting for someone else to confront me.

With my head down, I walked slowly to the shop, only to be greeted by another familiar voice. "Are you all right?" he said. I looked up and instantly recognized the face—it was my attacker. I nearly fainted from shock. Nothing prepared me for that moment as I struggled to compose myself. Different thoughts entered my head and again, I was in utter confusion. I did not know what to do, as I could feel the stares of people on me.

I continued walking, this time as fast as I could. I didn't give myself a chance to react, as I wasn't sure what I could do to this strapping man. I hated the look in his eyes, as it was a reminder of his casual approach to what he did to me. For him, it was business as usual as he wandered the streets in a carefree manner, while I was being tormented, scandalized and emotionally shackled by his violation. With my head still spinning and my eyes wet with tears, I went into the shop, bought my goods and was about to leave when an elderly man approached me. "Never mind, my child", he said. "You are too young for this to happen to you." He then walked away, shaking his head in disgust.

I was not only shocked but also dumbfounded. I looked at his concerned face and walked away feeling very embarrassed, yet strangely relieved that somebody was on my side. I went home with a feeling of bewilderment. Once again, I went to the cellar where I tried to come to terms with the events of the day.

CHAPTER SEVEN
Sunday Morning

I went to church as usual on Sunday morning, but I was extremely quiet. I didn't speak much. The whole Sunday was spent in grief, confusion and condemnation. I knew I loved the Lord, but I felt as if I'd messed up my life. I shouldn't have stood on the step. If I had gone into the shop with my cousins, then this would not have taken place. This should never have happened to a Christian because the Lord protects and keeps us safe. Why me?

I talked to God quietly and begged Him for forgiveness. "Please forgive me," I quietly prayed to myself. "Forgive me for the sin I committed last night. Forgive me for messing up my life. Help me that my good name would not be ruined because of this. Keep me safe and help me to cope at school tomorrow." I would have skipped school if I had a choice, but I had to go. There was no way of release, as I was always around people and could not even get space to think.

Everybody worshipped God joyfully that Sunday. The Youth Group was vibrant as they introduced a new way of worship to the church that was already steeped in traditional practices. The gifts of the Spirit were not acknowledged, and our presence created great unease among the leadership. It was the norm for the young people to speak in tongues, raise their hands, and praise God. Although the atmosphere was electrifying, we were seen as disruptive. The elders had been down once before to tell the young people to be quiet, and remind them that such conduct would not be tolerated. I didn't have the strength to raise my hands as I was trying to make sense of yesterday. Was it God's fault, his fault or my fault? Whose fault was it?

As I quietly tried to sort out the mess in my mind, I heard my name. "Can Sister Miney lead us in prayer?" I was called the Prayer Warrior at church. I couldn't preach, lead or sing but I could pray. I loved to pray, but this Sunday I didn't want to. There were too many things happening in my head for me to concentrate, and in a sense, I felt God had let me down. Why should I pray to Him if He couldn't even defend a helpless child like me?

I hesitated for a while. They're asking me to pray! Would God still hear my prayer? Will He answer me after what I had done yesterday? But hold on, I didn't do it; he did it to me. I was being punished for lack of knowledge and understanding. This torture would have been avoided, had somebody told me about "the birds and the bees," but life was too monotonous for anyone to think of such "trivial" issues. My mind was a clouded mess as I was unable to make sense of what was happening.

My sister, who was leading the worship, shouted my name again. "Can I ask Sister Miney to pray?" There was no getting away from it. If I didn't pray people would want to find out why, and my ordeal was too embarrassing to discuss with anyone. I held my breath for a while and muttered quietly to God, "I really don't want to pray today, but please help me."

I closed my eyes and raised my head to heaven, with tears rolling down my face. Interestingly, I prayed like I'd never prayed before. That Sunday, something happened to me. My prayer changed. I felt a burden for broken people, people who had been in the same situation as myself—the very poor, the lame, the battered, the bruised and children who had been messed up by circumstances like mine.

I prayed about poverty and social deprivation that people were trapped in. I prayed for all the children who were being hurt by other people, and I asked God to correct all the injustice in our community and speedily make all the wrongs right. My prayer was born out of frustration, anguish and a deep sense of sorrow for all the other Mineys out there.

After the prayer, I sat down and sobbed my heart out. All the young people were crying. Some were speaking in tongues, others were worshiping. God did a mighty work in the church. The elders could not stop us; we were overwhelmed by the presence of God. Although I felt like a weight had been lifted from off my shoulder, I was still painfully aware of the gossips surrounding my ordeal. For a brief moment, I felt that God was with me and He was going to see me through this difficult time. He didn't take away my ability to see visions and there was a sense of His power at work in my life.

I went home after church and was greeted with a barrage of quarreling from my grandmother. "You worthless child," she said. "You've got to tell me what happened. I thought you were a different child, but you're no better than the rest." My uncle's wife questioned me in a non-judgmental way, which gave me some form of consolation. Out of concern, my cousins queried my whereabouts on that fateful night.

My grandmother went on cursing for days trying to extract as much information as possible from me, but my lips remained sealed! At times, her language was colorful, and her insults stung like a swarm of angry bees attacking its victims. Somehow, I felt like I was being slowly and painfully ripped apart with a sharp knife, and there was no end to the torture. The wound was deeper than any physical pain anyone could inflict. I felt like I was trapped on an emotional roller coaster and couldn't get off.

Getting nowhere with her questions, grandmother—after throwing unkind words at me—approached me in a stern voice, "Miney!" I replied, "Yes ma'am." She then looked at me crossly and said, "I hope you're not carrying belly in my house." All of a sudden, the reality dawned on me. Not for one moment did I think about pregnancy. I could be pregnant! What he did to me could cause me to have a baby.

"Oh my God," I cried deep inside. What if I was "carrying belly," as my grandmother would say? I was already too squashed in the bed with my grandmother and my brother. Where would I put the baby? As space was already a problem, what would happen to the baby and me? I hated how my life was turning out. I wanted to leave home when I was older and enjoy a better lifestyle, not being stuck with a baby in tow! I started to pray, "God, not a baby." I sobbed and sobbed.

My baptism was a few days away and I was still in shock. Should I get baptized or not? How would I get out of this? By now, my white dress was already made. My other two sisters were also getting baptized and it was a big day for all of us. On a few occasions, I attempted to tell my minister what had happened but chickened out, as I was not sure how to explain my ordeal.

On Monday, as usual, I went to school which was about three and a half miles away. On my way I met my schoolmate, who also lived in the same community, very close to our home. We started talking as we usually did. As the conversation progressed, she paused and said, "I know what you did on Saturday night. You were caught with (let's call him Jack) doing it."

I nearly fainted. How on earth did she know? Who else knew? What was going to happen to my reputation? I paused, trying to contain myself. "Where did you hear that?" I asked, stuttering. She looked at me and said, "Almost everybody knows. Someone saw him pulling you down the steps and everyone knew what you were doing." I couldn't believe that almost everyone had heard about my plight in such a short space of time. EVERYONE KNOWS! What's going to happen—my baptism, my salvation and my life?

Over the next few days, I was bombarded with people prying for information. Some remarked how "naughty" I had been. The gossiping had spread both far and near, and I was the one being blamed for something I wasn't responsible for. My once good name was now full of mess and I detested it, but there was nothing I could do about it. Adults and young people alike were now aware that I was involved in the "dirtiest" act of my life, which left me open to ridicule and utter embarrassment.

I was now even more convinced that the guy standing on the road above must have seen what happened, as he was the voice on the other end of the door. Anger and humiliation nearly stifled me as I found myself in the center of a public disgrace. The callous stares from individuals and the haunting whispers from some of the older people sent cold chills through my body. Often times I watched my attacker carry on as normal. How dare he behave as if nothing had happened, when I was struggling to come to terms with this callous violation of my body! What he did deserved punishment, which was not yet forthcoming.

The thought of carrying a baby still plagued my mind, as I wasn't sure what to do. However, over the weeks I convinced myself that I was fine. Weeks later, we were introduced to Child Development lessons in school and one day I plucked up the courage to ask one of my teachers about sex education. She was a lovely lady who also led the Christian Fellowship, which I belonged to. I took the opportunity to ask as many questions as possible without referring to myself. After our discussion, I felt reassured and had a better understanding of what's involved in pregnancy, which later helped to put me out of my misery. It didn't take long before I discovered I wasn't expecting a baby. I was relieved at the prospect of not being a mother at such an early age.

At home, my only place of comfort was under the cellar. There I sat on a dusty piece of wood and prayed constantly, asking God to allow the young man, who may have seen my ordeal, to come forward. As the weeks rolled by, to my greatest horror and disappointment, he never did, and I was left alone to the mercy of my community. Had he come forward, I would have at least had been spared from the extra misery my community had imposed on me but, alas, this was not to be.

CHAPTER EIGHT
Good Friday

The day of my baptism had arrived and I had mixed feelings about it. I wasn't sure that I was doing the right thing because of my beastly encounter. I had no one to ask or even mention my plight to, and this left me in utter confusion. I was concerned about how people saw me and what God thought about me. Would He accept me or would He judge me for the wrong I had done? Should I be baptized, since I was so unclean?

The events of the last week were fresh in my mind and I was very angry. I was disgusted with myself for not going into the shop with my cousins. I felt as if I had put myself in the position to be abused, and I was to be blamed. Feelings of anger and hatred consumed me as I tried to make sense of my ordeal. I wasn't sure whether it was all right for me to feel this way, especially so close to my baptism. In my heart, I wanted to call it off, but I couldn't think of an excuse to tell my family, minister and friends.

By now, the incident had circulated around the whole community. Even in the adjacent districts, people were making derogatory comments about my behavior. I was shocked as to how many people knew about it. All the blame was geared towards me and there was no mention of the perpetrator's name. I was somehow this bad little girl who was responsible for an abuse that I didn't ask for. There was no justice in all of this. My once good name was now tarnished and no one was brought to accountability. How I wished there was someone who would come forward and talk in my defense.

It was about seven in the morning and my baptism was in two hours' time. The day before, many of the church members came to our house and prayed for us. We were told what to expect on the day and it sounded interesting, nevertheless I found it awkward because of my recent ordeal. My other two sisters were excited as they looked forward to a new life with Christ. At the meeting we were asked to give our testimonies, and my heart sank, as I wasn't sure of anything anymore. However, I reluctantly gave my testimony, which was sharp and to the point, and I was extremely glad when it was over.

By now I had made up my mind to be baptized, as there was no getting away from it. I knew I loved the Lord and wanted to follow Him, but I wasn't sure how much He loved me, especially after what happened last week. I immediately built up the courage and got ready for my journey to church. People were already gathering outside with their tambourines to march us down to the church, as was their normal custom. Those getting baptized were put in a line and escorted by the majority of the members, who sang choruses and knocked the tambourines. This was to be a public declaration of our intentions to follow Jesus.

My sisters and I were ready for our journey to the church. We were dressed in white knee-length dresses with white scarves. The look of innocence embraced us as we paraded the bumpy roads. Sister Janey was asked to pray and then the singing started; the tambourines, guitars and drums followed. As we marched down the road singing, "I have decided to follow Jesus, no turning back, no turning back," people came from everywhere and joined in the march. Others peered from their windows, and many stood at the side of the road and watched us as we made our way to the church for our baptism.

The church was steeped in traditional practices and these were upheld without anyone challenging them. One such practice was that candidates should not look behind them until the baptism was over, as there was a possibility that they would end up losing their faith. In obedience, we held our heads straight in front of us. We were also told not to wipe the water from our faces after emerging from the pool, or we would suffer the same consequences.

Once we arrived at church, we were seated on the front row and we were not allowed to look behind us. There was always somebody on hand that we could motion to if we needed any help, but our attention had to be focused ahead of us. This meant that we were serious about following Jesus. From the noise behind us, we could judge that church was packed with people. Baptisms on Good Friday were the norm in our community and people always looked forward to this occasion. It was one of the highlights, as relatives and friends arrived home from their jobs in Kingston to celebrate Easter with their families.

The service started and we were excited but nervous. I still wasn't sure whether I was doing the right thing, but there was no getting away from it now. Many songs were sung and it was a joyous occasion. Some of the young people were weeping as they praised God for His goodness and mercy. I also found myself crying in thankfulness and gratitude to God for saving me and keeping me sane at such a difficult time. I asked Him to help me to deal with all the things I had to cope with on my own. I told Him how embarrassed and angry I felt, with everyone having a negative image of me. I asked him for guidance regarding my future, as I wasn't sure where my life was heading.

It was now time for my baptism. The minister called my name. Three people had already been baptized and the atmosphere was electrifying. There were a lot of "Alleluias" and "Praise the Lord" as I walked slowly and cautiously to the baptismal pool. I remembered clearly that I shouldn't look behind me, so I kept my head in front of me. I was also worried that I would wipe the water from my face and be doomed to hell. I stepped into the pool with the help of our minister and deacon. At the request of my minister, I gave my testimony and prayed that everything would be all right.

My baptism took place and I was glad it was all over. After the baptism, the minister preached the sermon and we were served our first communion. At the end of the meeting, everyone came to congratulate us for the wonderful step we had taken. I responded cautiously, wondering if they knew of my unfortunate experience. This was now an opportunity to prove myself and show the community that I wasn't guilty of committing a crime, but would they take me seriously?

CHAPTER NINE
Living a Nightmare

The baptism had passed but I was in the same predicament. I was none the wiser than before my baptism. I felt like I was living in a vacuum and no one really and truly understood my emotional state. I was being tainted for something I was not responsible for and life had become a living nightmare.

The crude comments and the smart remarks about my ordeal were tearing my life apart. My activities in church were now shrouded with doubt and distrust, and I felt as though I hadn't been taken seriously. God was still real to me, but at times I had mixed feelings about Him, even though I was conscious that, had it not been for His help, I might have had a nervous breakdown.

I continued to live this nightmare for a long time, and at times, my life seemed empty and torturous. My desire for a better way of life was overwhelming, but the odds were cruelly stacked against me. I felt that poverty had blinded many people's eyes, and their continuous struggle for survival had stopped them from seeing the important things in life. No child should be victimized or abused without a public outcry, else all children would be put at risk. In my case, I was left open to continuous abuse, as there was hardly anyone to protect my innocence.

I longed for my ordeal to be over but there was no sign of it ever happening. Every step I took, I was reminded of what I was supposed to have done wrong, and oftentimes I had to sternly rebuke myself for taking the blame. There were occasions when I wasn't sure whose fault it was, as the finger of accusation had always been pointed in my direction. I was pronounced guilty on every charge and sentenced to untold misery and torment from my community. Hopefully common sense would prevail one day. Please God, let it be sooner than later, was my familiar prayer.

At school, there were constant reminders from my peers that I wasn't really what I had portrayed. I was seen as both deceptive and fake. It was difficult for me to move on, as my whole life was overshadowed with this sorry affair. I couldn't make sense of the whole scenario and my childish mind had restrained me from a sensible explanation.

The mere fact that an adult could forcibly invade the privacy of a young, unsuspecting thirteen-year-old child without a public outcry was a great injustice. Greater still was the fact that she was the one on trial. When a society reaches that demoralizing depth, where the perpetrator walks free and an innocent child is punished, there is something sadly wrong.

With all the setbacks, I continued living my Christian life to the best of my ability. There were times when I failed miserably, and in my search for love and assurance, I made mistakes, but my whole desire was to see this thing through. Maybe God had something better at the end of this seemingly needless ordeal. I became involved in many activities, including visiting the sick and holding street meetings although, for me, our first meeting on the street was a disaster. Not only did this incident fracture my heart, but it also left me with incredible pain and discomfort for a long time.

Our first meeting was scheduled to take place in our hometown. I became increasingly uncomfortable with the whole idea. For me, this was a place of pain, torment and the greatest betrayal I had experienced in my short life. What could I possibly tell people about Jesus, when I felt so bad about myself? Poverty still had a firm grip on my life, and the abuse had left me vulnerable. What on earth was I supposed to say to those people who seemed to condone wrongdoing and victimize the innocent? There was nothing but contempt for those who knew my situation and further persecuted me, while the perpetrator walked free with a spring in his step.

It was hard to move on from the place of anguish and disappoint-ment, as there was no outlet for my frustration. I had no choice but to still pass him on the street, and even communicate with him as if nothing had happened to me, although I was hurting badly inside. The ordeal became like a rope around my neck and was strangling me.

Although I was confused to the core, I still loved Jesus. In fact, I now understand that He was the one that had kept me sane over the years. Each day, God gave me fresh visions, which were full of hope and inspira-tions. Great comfort was found in Bible reading and praying and helping people when I could. My life slowly began to change when I realized that I couldn't sort out the problems on my own. With this realization, I handed over my problems one by one to Him. Each day He reassured me of His love with these simple, yet profound words '*I love you.*' He was the only one I could talk to about what I was going through. My pain was far too deep and personal to share with anyone else.

The day finally came for our first street meeting. Everyone was excited about our venture, and all the members of our group helped to set up our table and lamp. It was interesting to see the small square packed with people in a very short space of time. This wasn't unusual, as people were always searching for answers to their problems. Among the crowd was my attacker, who sat on the wall, smiling as if he was the king of the jungle. It had only been a short time since he molested me, and here I was about to testify about the goodness of God.

We started the service by singing many choruses and knocking our tambourines. The scripture was read and soon it was time to share our testimonies. One by one, the young people testified, followed by other Christians from the audience. To my dismay, I felt as if I was being viciously pushed out on a limb as they affirmed their faith in Christ. Although they did not deliberately intend to hurt me, a feeling of being caught in a trap haunted me. Some of the testimonies of the young people from neighboring churches went something like this: "I thank God I can stand in my own district and say that Jesus saves, He keeps, He satisfies. Today it's a privilege to be here standing before you all where nobody or no man can say anything about me. Please pray for me in Jesus' name."

As I listened to the testimonies, time stood still for a moment as my mind raced back to that fateful day. From the corner of my eye, I glimpsed my abuser sporting a massive smile over his hairy face. For a brief second, I almost lost my composure, as I watched myself in my mind's eye approaching this hefty-looking man and beating him to a pulp. By the time I came back to myself, my hands were clenched tightly in a fist, and my frail body had become rigid from the intense anger and hatred I felt for him. Confusion shattered my world, as I wasn't sure I was allowed to feel that way. Was I intended to feel any hurt or resentment or was I supposed to exude love and forgiveness? What was I supposed to feel or do? To be honest, I wasn't sure. After all, I was a Christian.

The testimonies forced home the sad reality that I could never again stand in my district and testify that no man knew anything about me. In fact, he was sitting only a few yards from me and had never been apprehended for his crime. I fought hard to hold back the tears as I stepped forward to give my testimony. I wanted so desperately to share the same testimony as my other colleagues, but my circumstances had stopped me.

There was a hushed silence as I moved to the front. To me, it seemed like everyone was waiting in eager anticipation to hear what this naughty little teenager was about to say. Sheer determination urged me on, and in a resounding voice I testified something that went like this: "I thank God for saving and keeping me. If it weren't for Him, I don't know what I would do or where I would be. One songwriter said, 'I want to go home, to live with my Savior and King. When I look back in life and see what a failure life brings, I wonder why God made me living in this world of sorrow and shame.' Please pray for me in Jesus' name."

As I finished, there were a lot of amens. After the service, a woman in her early fifties called me and shook my hand. Speaking aloud for everyone to hear, she blurted out impolitely, "Miney's testimony was the only real testimony, the others were rubbish." She let go of my hand and walked off, shouting "Hypocrites!" To this day, I am not sure why she came to that conclusion. However, my own thoughts interpreted her actions to mean that, maybe God had a special purpose for my life. She had obviously heard the gossip, and maybe she felt sorry for me when she saw how frail I looked.

CHAPTER TEN
A Shattered Hope

Despite the hell I went through, my time in the Young People's group was very rewarding. We rapidly grew in number and were later called the Mt. Industry Evangelistic Team. Lin, my older sister, was elected as the team leader and she was excellent at leadership. Not only did she preach the gospel and teach Bible studies but she also trained us to believe in ourselves and reach for the impossible. All of us were given opportunities to develop our potential and launch out in our areas of ministry. It was interesting to see everyone in our group taking part in different activities. There was no place for the shy or coward as Lin believed in group participation and that everyone had something to offer.

Our ministry took us far and near and we visited many churches preaching and teaching the word of God. On many occasions, we reached out to the poor in our community offering financial help from money raised from concerts, cleaning their houses and preparing meals. We also raised funds for repairs on the houses of some of the elderly people. We ministered in neighboring districts where we were called to pray for the sick, conduct funeral services and deal with problems in relationships. For a while, our group became a symbol of hope for the hopeless as we were bombarded with different kinds of requests. There was a sense of fulfillment in that area of ministry and I felt happy helping people.

With the help of our minister Reverend Davidson, our Evangelistic Team grew from strength to strength. Our lives were now focused on ministering to people and spending time together supporting and encouraging each other. Reverend Davidson was a kind, caring and energetic young minister in his late twenties when he became involved with our church. He was like a breath of fresh air to our community. Because of his love, compassion and willingness to reach out to the poor, everyone loved and respected him. Although he was in charge of three other churches, he still found time to visit the sick and isolated. Life with our minister was interesting as he got our group actively involved in funerals, weddings, counseling and administering communion to the housebound. Although it was exciting helping the most vulnerable in our community, there were times when I still felt overwhelmed with my ordeal. However, this was to be our greatest training ground and we soon developed new skills on how to minister more effectively to the needs of the sick and oppressed.

Although nothing much had changed in my life, I had a better relationship with God, and for some unknown reason I felt a greater passion to help the weak and oppressed. My prayer life had blossomed and I spent many days thanking God for His goodness and telling Him about my struggles. Poverty and oppression were still my greatest enemies and I detested them in every way. The rape ordeal continued to haunt me and every now and then, I retreated in my own little private world, snapping at everyone and crying uncontrollably.

Secondary school was sometimes daunting as I was an average student with only a few good friends. I became an active member of the School's Youth Fellowship and attended regular prayer sessions and Bible studies. Our Evangelistic Team had made a great impact on my life and, as my confidence grew, I slowly began to share my dreams and visions with my classmates.

Even though my spiritual life was blooming, there were times I still felt like I was on an emotional roller coaster. At times I seemed to cope very well, whilst at other times I felt broken and defeated. I felt torn between my faith, poverty and my rape ordeal and I wasn't sure if it was all right for me to feel this way. Both excitement and grief mingled with each other as I served God and watched our parents struggle to make ends meet.

It was a constant struggle for us as my sister and I had to go to the fields early in the morning, either to chop canes or dig produce from the soil, in readiness for my mother's market day. After carrying the heavy load in the heat, we then had to get ready for our three-mile trip to school. Our journey was long and arduous and we ran most of the way to avoid being caned viciously by the principal for being late. If caught we were left black and blue from the severe beatings, or we were left to stand in the glaring sun, possibly to suffer from heatstroke. There was hardly any room for sympathy or explanation and yet again, this had become another devastating pattern in our lives. We were no strangers to emotional and physical abuse, which I very much detested, but we were unable to do anything about it. How I wished I could explain to the teacher the reasons for us being late, to avoid being frequently caned. Would it really have made a difference anyway? We were far too poor for anyone to take us seriously, and besides, no one would be interested in what we had to say.

The rape ordeal continued to be a major factor in my life as I had been unsuccessful in sharing it with my family, although attempts had been made on several occasions. Unfortunately, I had never been able to move on, as I was always reminded of my past.

Through some strange coincidence, I met the person who had walked me home after the abuse on that horrendous night. We became good friends and communicated on a fairly regular basis, which I found very helpful. We exchanged letters and spent time chatting about life, whenever he was able to visit from Kingston. For the first time, I was able to slowly let someone into my dark and haunted arena, as I shared some of my frustrations with him. This gave me a feeling of overwhelming relief, as I felt I was being listened to and taken seriously. Oh, how I desperately wanted this to continue. I wanted to express my pains so badly to someone who was non-judgmental, and who would reassure me that everything was going to be all right.

There were a lot of things I needed to clarify about my life. It was imperative for me to make some sense of the emotional aspect of my life and how best to deal with my sexual nightmare. I needed to understand why things seemed to be working against me, as everything I put my hands to seemed to come back to haunt me. Out of anguish, I sat down and wrote this young man a letter, expressing how I was feeling, and the trauma I was going through. I disclosed other personal details to him about my ordeal, which would be classed by my grandmother as "inappropriate." These were the type of things that were regarded as "taboo" in our family, but I felt he was one person I could talk to, as he was somewhat aware of my predicament.

Being very immature, I put the letter in my grandmother's over-crowded room, hiding it as securely as possible. Days later I discovered that it had gone missing. My prayers now became a matter of urgency. "Please God, please, please don't let grandma find the letter." "Let it be that I have misplaced it so that I can be spared any added torment in my life." It didn't take long before grandma came facing me like an angry lion. She had found my letter and I was left feeling crushed to the bones. This was the start of another nightmare. Grandmother saw my letter, and although she couldn't read or write, she ripped it open and got my uncle to read it to both her and his wife. My uncle's wife saw the funny side to it and with a mischievous twinkle in her eyes she laughed uncontrollably. As she enjoyed the moment of shock and disbelief, she looked at me and said, "Miney, how you so bad?" My uncle and grandma, however, remained as serious as a judge as they expressed their anger and disappointment. Needless to say, I went through "hell and high waters." The quarreling and the arguments were consistent as this again confirmed that I was this little, naughty, no-good child who had only one thing on my mind—men. All I was searching for was someone I could trust to share my pains. This was a desperate cry for help, which was unfortunately short-lived.

After going through weeks of mental torture, I decided to try again. I desperately needed an outlet for my pains and frustrations, as this was driving me crazy. I had discovered that there was release in sharing my feelings and there was no stopping now. The second letter I wrote was more or less the same as the previous one. This time I asked my neighbor to post it three miles away, but to my utter disbelief, the letter got lost and arrived in the hands of the young man's mother!

She was one of the prominent members of our community and this was about to destroy my already shattered life. I later learned that the information had spread like wildfire around the adult community. My life had now been weighed in a balance and I was found wanting. My quest for answers and release from my burdens had further damaged my already tainted reputation. There was no refuge for my soul, no escape from my pain and no release from captivity. By now I was nothing but a mental outcast in people's minds. That was to be the last time I saw the young man in a long while, although we bumped into each other on the odd occasion. I was once again left to sort out my mess on my own.

CHAPTER ELEVEN
A Facial Disfigurement

My life remained bleak for a long time. Nothing much changed, except things steadily got worse as the years rolled by. My entire life seemed to revolve around searching for answers to my problems, and seeking an early escape from the hardship I had been experiencing. By now, my sleep had been severely disrupted and I felt like I was on the verge of slowly losing my sanity. The nightmares became more frequent and disturbing dreams about my past awakened me. Most nights were spent awake, tossing and turning and feeling sorry for myself. I was mentally and physically exhausted and at times my head felt as if it was going to explode.

Somehow, I felt as if I was in the lion's den ready to be ripped into shreds by its paws, as one thing after the other invaded my life. I was now fourteen years old with teenage spots all over my face and this added another strain to my life. My entire face was covered with acne and I felt like an outcast. All the creams I used failed to make any difference, and this made me feel worse about myself. Constant reminders of my ugliness made my life difficult. Unable to live down my past ordeal, prayer and daily conversations with God became my only means of comfort.

Besides all the torment, I was still active in church. I continued to share my faith with others, attended all the group meetings and was involved in evangelism. I developed a desire to help and protect the vulnerable and I was always willing to run errands for the poor and offer help to whomever I could. My life was busy and I immersed myself in different activities in the hope that I would somehow forget my ghastly experiences. At fifteen years old, I became a Sunday School teacher and I was extremely happy to work with the children. Sunday School was good and for once I felt like I was getting some form of control of my life. As I watched the children enjoy their young lives I felt a sense of duty to protect and shield them from the same fate I suffered, but I wasn't sure how. A feeling of being cheated of my youth frequently visited me and many times, I had to stop myself from screaming. Deep down I was tearing up inside and I didn't know how to stop it.

Although my life was far from being perfect, I was given opportunities at church to conduct morning worship and lead Bible studies. Even though I was hesitant at times, I made an effort to try. As time went by, my abilities to lead and counsel became evident and this attracted people both in and around the community. Very soon, both the young and old were discussing their problems with me. Some of the problems included physical and sexual abuse, problems in relationships and child abuse. I spent many days visiting individuals in their homes and talking to children about their plights. Somehow, I could empathize with them, as I wasn't any better off myself. I felt somewhat fulfilled in this area of ministry.

At the age of sixteen, my life was about to suffer another devastating blow. I awoke one night with a terrible and excruciating pain in my face and jaw. It felt like both a headache and toothache. For a while, I wasn't sure what was happening as I struggled to find some relief before waking my grandmother. My night was sleepless and I screamed in agony from the intense discomfort. Everyone searched for and administered home remedies, but to no avail. Nothing helped, and by the following morning, the right side of my face was so swollen that I could barely see.

With a white scarf around my face, I was taken to the doctor to seek medical advice. There was only one bus, which was very unreliable, that passed through our community. That day I prayed earnestly for the bus to arrive, as there were no other means of transportation. We waited for a long time and thankfully the bus arrived. It was packed to its fullest capacity, with three or four people sitting on one seat designed to accommodate two people. The space for standing passengers was already overcrowded. There was hardly any room left for anyone; however, people were determined to get to their destinations and they clambered for even a foot space on the bus.

Despite being in excruciating pain and suffering from sheer exhaustion, I managed to scramble to the first step on the bus, only to be pushed savagely inside until I was stuck in the midst of the already crammed mass of people. Unfortunately, only one of my feet had reached the floor of the bus, while the other one was stuck somewhere between the people and could not reach the floor.

The pain became even more intense as people's faces rubbed against my already swollen and painful face. I had no choice but to travel to the doctor about twelve miles away, standing on one foot. How I managed to endure the pain, discomfort and trauma of that day, only God knew.

The doctor examined me and gave me a letter of admission to the hospital. I arrived at the hospital, feeling tearful and upset, only to be met by some unpleasant nurses in white uniform. Life for the nurses was hard as they struggled to make ends meet. Many were cheerful and friendly, while some were very cold and callous, and unfortunately, the poorer patients became the scapegoats for their frustration.

Beatings, insults and neglect appeared to be the norm, as some elderly people in excruciating pain were pitilessly slapped and told to be quiet. There was hardly any mercy or compassion from some of the nurses, from this so-called 'caring' environment. Instead, we found ourselves in a chamber of torment. I managed to make friends with one of the patients, a lovely middle-aged lady who I called Miss Lee. She was pleasant and caring and had a special love for me. Although she was ill, she always looked out for me and made sure I was all right. She was like a mother and I loved and respected her. Many of our days were spent chatting and she tried her best to cheer me up when I was down.

My condition deteriorated in the hospital and my face had crystallized into a stone-hard lump. It was so swollen that I was barely able to see out of my right eye and hardly able to open my mouth. As I was unable to eat anything solid I had to resort to a straw for fluid intake. The doctors were baffled at my deterioration, as they weren't sure what the diagnosis was. Initially, they said it was an abscess in my face, but to my utter amazement, I heard words flying around from both visitors and nurses that there was a possibility it could be cancer.

I wasn't sure what to believe as people speculated openly on what my condition might be. If the lump on my jaw was caused from an abscess, why wasn't anything being done about it? I thought to myself. One elderly friend came to see me and told me that he thought I had cancer, as the symptoms were similar to that of his sister who later died from the condition. People's speculation and indiscretion were tearing my life apart. In the end, I was reluctant to see anyone due to their level of insensitivity. Their crude remarks were of no consolation to me, as I was already in a state of panic. However, my newfound friend encouraged and supported me through this time of difficulty.

One day, Miss Lee wasn't feeling very well and she was unable to eat. It was obvious that something was wrong, as she wasn't talking as much as she used to. She was reluctant to call the nurses, as they were sometimes rude and ill mannered, but I went and called one of them for assistance. A nurse returned and spoke to her harshly, commanding her to have her meal, but she was too weak to even lift her hand.

She sat in the chair looking frail and limp, and I kept praying that God would sustain and keep her well. I felt both awful and helpless, as I wasn't able to help Miss Lee in her time of need. How I wished I was able to hold her and tell her that everything would be all right, but the sad and empty look in her eyes told me otherwise. As she sat in the armchair looking weak and shaken, she slowly lifted her head and looked at me with a faint smile on her face. It was as if she wanted to tell me not to worry.

Minutes later, Miss Lee fell forward in her chair, and one of the nurses ran to help her. By this time, I was in tears, as I knew that something was terribly wrong with my friend. To my utter amazement, what I heard next had me in a state of shock for the next few minutes. As the nurse surged forward to assist Miss Lee, the other nurse shouted back, "Leave her alone, she is only pretending." With this, Miss Lee fell forward, falling off the chair onto the floor. Minutes later, she died. I was horrified at the level of negligence in the hospital. Other patients watched in disbelief while the two nurses had a haunted look over their faces, but none of us said a word, for fear of being the next.

My days were tearful and empty and I felt I had no fight left in me. I desperately wanted to go home. It was impossible for me to live with this added nightmare. My only friend had just died through negligence and I was unable to do anything about it. As her beautiful daughters arrived at her bedside, I felt a sense of duty to tell them what had happened, but I was fearful of the repercussions.

At sixteen years old, this was all too much for me to take in. Sadness and intense pain overwhelmed me as I tried to make sense of her sudden death. I was now alone, left to dry my own tears and suffer in silence again. There was now no one to hold my hands when I felt sad and no one's bed to climb into whenever I was in pain. With my face swollen and disfigured, the intense feeling of loneliness and despondency once again crossed my path. I was scared of the prospect of losing my sight and I was afraid that my mouth wouldn't be able to open properly again. It was sheer hell trying to contain my emotions, knowing that my friend had died through carelessness.

I never knew what exactly killed her, but I believed that the fall had contributed to her sudden death. My heart was shattered as I watched the porters taking Miss Lee out covered with a white sheet. As her body was carried past my bed, with my face drenched with tears, I tearfully mouthed, Thank you Miss Lee and Good-bye. Choking back the tears I managed to whisper, I am so sorry Miss Lee, before she was whisked down the corridor, out of sight.

I missed my friend badly and I wanted desperately to talk to her and tell her how much I appreciated her kindness and how sorry I was, but she was gone. I felt all-alone with my pain and frustration. There was no one to check on me in the nights and offer hope and encouragement. Here I was again, all alone with my thoughts, and I wasn't sure how to cope with the added heartache. Again, that feeling of despondency accompanied me wherever I went. The hospital became a constant reminder of brutality and death. I didn't feel safe anymore and I mourned the loss of my friend for a long time. The pain in my face was excruciating, and as the weeks rolled by, there was no sign of improvement.

I stayed in the hospital for a few weeks. When all the medications failed to work, I was sent home worse than when I went in, with a massively disfigured face and a half-blinded right eye. On leaving the hospital, the doctor's last words to my mother were, "I'm sorry, we have done our best, and there is nothing more we can do."

After all I had been through, I was now left with a disfigured face that the doctors couldn't fix. My friend had just died and I was devastated. The massive lump on my face was yet another obstacle to overcome. Everything seemed determined to rip my already shattered life apart and my heart became tormented with crushing and unbearable pain.

I found it almost impossible to cope. I could hide the emotional scars to some extent, but the lump on my face was visible for everyone to see. My right eye was almost closed and my mouth was now leaning to one side due to the massive swelling. It was a gruesome sight and very scary, as the side of my face became rock hard. The memories of Miss Lee remained in my thoughts; however, they were stained with great sadness. If she were still here with us she would have held my hand and said, jokingly, "Child, don't be worried about your pretty face, because it will soon be better, and don't go crying out all your tears as if there won't be any tomorrow." With this she would have thrown her firm arms around me and laughed.

Another three months went by, with frequent visits to the hospital without any progress, until a minister from America visited one of our neighboring churches. During his visit, I attended one of the meetings and sat at the back of the church. Being conscious about my facial disfigurement, I held my head down to avoid the stares from other people. After delivering his message, he called a few people to the front and prayed for them, and many were healed of their sicknesses. During his prayer time, he paused and said, " There is a young lady at the back with a swelling on her right jaw. God wants to heal you, just make your way to the front and I will pray for you." Not only was I shocked but I was also terrified. I could not understand how he knew I was there as I had never stood up once in the service, and it was impossible for him to see me, while sitting down. With all these questions going around in my head, I carefully looked around to see if anyone was going forward, but no one did. Again, he repeated his call, saying, the young lady is here and she is sitting at the back. God knows who you are and He knows about all your pains and heartache.

This time, I was convinced that the call was for me, and I made my way slowly to the altar. As soon as the minister saw me he said, " You are the one." I was now in no doubt that God was looking out for me. All along, He had been there helping me through my struggles and willing me to carry on. The minister then prayed and told me that in about five days, God would begin the healing process in my life. I went home feeling happier than I had been in a long time. There was a sense of anticipation in the air as I looked forward to my miracle.

Each day was filled with a strange type of excitement as I literally counted down the days. True to his word, on the fifth day, a boil appeared on my right jaw. It was weird, looking at this horrible-looking boil on top of the large swelling already on my face, but I couldn't wait to see what would happen next.

Over the next few days, the boil ruptured and that was the start of the healing process. As the pus drained from my face, the swelling slowly decreased and I was able to see a little better. During this time, there were many embarrassing moments as pus was always leaking from my face; sometimes whilst in the company of my friends, on the bus, during dinner, on the street, in fact, everywhere I went. This was yet another mountain to climb. This process took another few weeks, and although I had improved, I was left with a lopsided face and a sunken jaw. God had again shown me His mercy and I was grateful for His healing power.

The improvement to my face boosted my confidence, although I still had a long way to go. I was now beginning to make short journeys to the shop and had visited church a few times. Church was extremely supportive and many people visited my home and prayed for me. During this time people continued to share their problems with me. I listened intently and offered the advice I felt necessary at the time. There were children who wanted to leave home; some felt they were treated unfairly while others felt trapped by their circumstances. There were others who only wanted Bible studies and encouragement and I was only too happy to assist. With all that was happening, I couldn't get away from the ongoing emotional pain from my ordeal, which still haunted me, but there was no alternative but to carry on the best way I could. Although God was slowly healing my face, I still felt sensitive about my appearance.

This led me to visit an optician, to whom I explained my situation. After much persuasion on my part, he finally prescribed a pair of glasses, although my sight was in good condition. At eighteen years old, I took the opportunity to purchase a pair of glasses with a large frame, in the hope they would cover my facial scar. I wore the glasses for about eight years, which helped to further boost my confidence.

I was hesitant to return to secondary school for an extra year, as I would be the oldest child in the school, at the ripe old age of eighteen—how humiliating! Despite my protest, my mother insisted I return to school to catch up on the year that I had missed. This resulted in me being placed with a class of seventeen-year-olds, as all my classmates had already graduated from the school. Initially this eroded my confidence and gave me a feeling of unease and distress, but I continued to attend.

CHAPTER TWELVE
An Invitation to England

My extra year at secondary school proved to be an eventful one. During the course of the year, I competed in a national essay competition and gained second place. I received a prize of thirty dollars and a return plane trip to Montego Bay. It was a very exciting time for me, as my pictures were in the national newspaper and the prize giving was televised. I felt very special, as I became a celebrity for a short period, both in my school and district.

This was indeed a great accomplishment. There was now something positive in my life that I could talk about. For a while, all the negative experiences became strangely insignificant as I wallowed in self-pride and satisfaction. Life became more pleasant and appealing, and the small fragrance of achievement gave me an appetite for knowledge. Studying much harder than I usually did became a pleasurable activity and reading books became a newfound hobby.

My past ordeal was no longer the main focus in my life. This minor achievement taught me that there was the possibility of a brighter future, and despite my ordeal, I could still be happy. My happiness was therefore dependent on the decisions that I make about my life. All that was necessary was a desire to at least try and see beyond my pain. Interestingly, this revelation enabled me to understand that I didn't have to continue to live with a victim mentality. I could use my trauma in a positive way to help others. What a new discovery it was to learn that nobody could make me happy, except me. I realized that my experiences were only a fragment of myself, they weren't the real me and there was much more to my life than my ordeals. This was a startling revelation. The more I thought about it, the more I realized how suppressed I had been because of my negative encounters.

It was an interesting voyage, as I made attempts to discover the true me. It was empowering to discover that I was someone of worth and integrity, someone who is loveable and capable of radiating Christ, even through the very shadows of bewilderment and torment. It was imperative for me to understand that my past did not dictate my future.

After leaving school, I was offered a job at the Mount Industry Primary School while attending an in-service training course to develop my teaching skills. This was interesting and rewarding as I was able to relate to children who were struggling one way or another, and offer any practical help where possible. My facial disfigurement had always been a point for ridicule and mockery but as time went on, I slowly began to gain more confidence. Although I had many setbacks, I was determined not to live in my past.

Life had become somewhat more manageable as I was beginning to think more positively. I was also in a position of responsibility and earning a small income, which made a huge difference financially. However, my nightmare hadn't stopped. There was yet another difficult hurdle to overcome, as I was now teaching next door to my abuser. Although the years had passed, seeing him regularly was a constant reminder of the event that took place about five years ago. I was angry and bitter as there was no apology or remorse and I hated him for destroying my reputation, however, due to the nature of the job, I had no choice but to communicate on a professional level. Nevertheless, this was difficult as there had been no closure to the ongoing torment; but I was determined to at least try and get on with my life.

By now, I understood that what he had done was not my fault. *He was the abuser and I was an innocent child,* who was made to carry the guilt around for many years without being vindicated. This made me furious, as I had unnecessarily blamed myself for his violation. It was hard to rid myself of the constant ridicule from members of my community and even the teachers from the school, who continually made me feel I was responsible for the abuse. I felt that there was no way of escape as I was often told I was no angel. While I was suffering the consequence of his action, there was no punishment on his part and he was, in fact, made to feel that his actions had been justified. Although I had made a decision not to live in my past, I realized it wasn't going to be easy.

Poverty and deprivation continued to parade itself on our streets and in our homes. The roads had become worse from wear and tear, there was still no means of proper running water, and people's lives had become static in terms of destitution. There was no future for this forgotten district, although our small community had produced some of the most talented and professional people. Because of the lack of job opportunities, there had always been a steady migration of people from the rural to the urban areas in search of jobs and a better lifestyle. For that reason most of my friends had left, and I too, longed to leave and start a new life.

My desire to escape was unbearable. Although I was now working as a teacher, I found myself being traumatized by my mother's new job. She was working at the same school where I was teaching, sweeping the schoolyard and cleaning the classrooms. Embarrassment and sadness gnawed at me as I watched her clean the school, from the dusty yard to the windows, very often being cloaked in dust. How I wished that the ground would open up and swallow me at times, or I would be wrenched from planet Earth to a place where no one knew me. It was hard to conceal my pain and embarrassment, as I saw her on a daily basis working so hard for a meager salary that was not enough to survive on. Watching my mother doing her job brought home the brutal reality that my fight against this social disease called poverty was going to be long and arduous. To me, she became a symbol of oppression as she fought for survival.

I lived this nightmare for another five years with no reprieve, until I was invited to England in 1984. I arrived on August 5 and studied Christian education for a while. I desperately wanted an answer for the torment that had so brutally robbed me of my innocence. I needed an understanding from God about the injustice and oppression that certain people faced in their lifetime. One of my ways of obtaining such knowledge was through the Bible.

Life in England was incredibly hard and at first, the country did not live up to my expectations. However, I was grateful for the opportunity to at least rid myself of some of the emotional shackles that had bound me. There were no streets paved with gold as I had been led to believe, but there was comfort in knowing I could again live in peace without the finger of accusation being pointed in my direction. Hopefully, this would at least give me some respite from my gruesome ordeal and the torturous remarks from my colleagues.

Soon after arriving in England, I realized that there were many new obstacles to deal with. Not only did I have to adjust to a new culture but I also had to deal with racism. The way of life was completely different and it was a struggle to get used to the differences that existed. Things like people's accents, humor and expressions were difficult to understand. The weather was a massive culture shock and the winter, accompanied with frost and snow, was hard to get used to. However, with time I soon learned to cope with my new way of life.

The houses, especially the terraced ones, took me aback. It was incredible seeing those buildings for the first time. Out of ignorance, one could easily confuse them for factories because of how close they were to each other, yet the inside was most times pleasant and beautiful. The double-decker buses were another point of interest and I relished the idea of traveling on the top floor. These differences fascinated me and I was interested to see as much of the country as possible. England is an interesting country and although it can be damp and cold, it has many positive aspects to it.

Whilst studying, I met Sandra Jones and Charlene Larrier. Sandra moved to Harborne after studying at university in Leicester. We shared a room and developed a strong friendship over the years. She became a great source of encouragement and support and God used her to touch my life as she offered both practical and financial help. She continues to be a faithful friend, always ready to make a difference in people's lives.

Through Sandra, I had the opportunity of meeting Charlene, her cousin. We developed a fruitful relationship and shared many good times together. She has always been consistent, supportive and encouraging. Thank God for using her to touch my life.

I studied under severe hardship, yet God had been faithful in meeting my needs and bringing the right people in my path. Money was scarce and it was difficult coping with the damp weather. There were times when the weather proved intolerable, especially during the winter season when there was heavy snowfall on the ground. The cold was extremely hard to adjust to and it didn't take long before I started to suffer from some of the effects of it. I missed the sunshine greatly and often would exchange anything to be in the sun.

My first winter in England was an adventure as I traveled from Walsall to Harborne in the heavy snowfall. Not only had the weather filled me with both fear and excitement, but also I was anxious to try out my winter boots, which I had earlier bought. Seeing the snow for the first time was like a dream come true, yet the thought of traveling in it filled me with apprehension, as I wasn't sure what to expect.

After putting on my long woolly socks, I finally made my way out and was greeted not only by snow, but also the most ferocious wind I had encountered in my new country. It stung my face like angry bees causing me to run into a few shops asking for confirmation on whether the white fluff falling from the sky was really snow. I was often reassured with a smile and told that that was indeed part of the winter weather in England. With great difficulty, I managed to get on the bus with my ears, hands and feet numb and my whole body shivering uncontrollably.

After getting off the bus into the high snow, I soon discovered that my boots were unsuitable for the weather. Every few steps I made greeted me with shock and disbelief as both my boots had fallen off and were left in the snow. Unfortunately, the back of the boots had pressed down to the heel because they were slightly too small for my feet, and they were, in fact, summer boots. With tears running down my cheeks that frequently turned into loud sobs on the street, I repeatedly placed my boots on my feet only to have them dragged off again by the high snow. My screams were loud as frustration got the better of me. A few people came to my aid but were unsuccessful. One couple suggested that I tied the lace around my feet, but the snow soon callously ripped it off. My entire journey revolved around walking a few steps forward and taking many steps backward to search for my boots. This was far from amusing and one of my worst ordeals.

Life in England was turning into a nightmare, as I had to deal with the cultural differences and struggle to make ends meet. It was difficult to pay for college fees and find money for rent and heating. There were times when I felt that I had been permanently stalked by poverty, and to some extent, I could understand it in my own country; but for the same fate to befall me in a European country was beyond understanding. However, I believe God was still in control and was always with me even in the difficult times. He had indeed sent Sandra and Charlene at the right time to meet some of my most desperate needs, which they did without grumbling.

It is gratifying to recall the many times God had proven Himself to me, even during my time at college. Later, I enrolled as a student at Springdale College. Having no money, I stepped out in faith, and told the principal I would have my college fees ready as soon as possible. There was no other alternative but to pray and believe that God, who supplies all my needs, would look after me financially. It didn't take long before God intervened, because that very day, He lovingly and graciously met my needs.

Just about the same time I was praying, God was speaking to four people about my situation. It is satisfying to know that God really cares about us and His timing is always perfect in meeting us at the point of our needs. The telephone rang, and the voice on the other end of the line said, "Almina, we were praying today, and the Lord spoke to us and told us to pay your fees for the year." Before they could finish their statement, I shouted out, "Alleluia, thank you Jesus!"

I explained to them that I was just on my knees praying about my college fees, as they were due for payment shortly, and how grateful I was for their obedience to God. That was the beginning of greater things in my life. Over the next few days, I had been astonished at God's favor, as people began to touch my life in many different ways. A couple from my local church approached me and said that God had told them to give me five pounds weekly until the end of the college year, while another couple bought me groceries every week. I can't forget these miracles as God had met all my needs throughout that year. All praise and thanks to Him.

CHAPTER THIRTEEN
Shaking Hands with Destiny

Over the years, I have frequently asked myself these questions. " Who am I?" "What am I doing here and what is my purpose in life?" Somehow, life would have become more relevant if I understood the reasons for my existence. It is therefore important for every individual to know his or her purpose in life, because knowing our purpose will undoubtedly align us with our destiny. Despite all the upheavals we have encountered, there is a place of safety in knowing who we are and to whom we belong. This chapter reveals how people and events had been instrumental in bringing me closer to my destiny.

Life's challenges can often bring us face to face with our Creator, who is the answer to our existence. When we have been pushed way beyond our limitations, there is only one place left to seek refuge, and that is in God. This is often a reminder that there is someone out there that is greater than us. He has total control over the universe but He is also interested in every aspect of our lives. His ultimate plan and purpose is to make Himself known, in order to point us towards our destiny. I have had many experiences that I can only attribute to God, who is always trying to get my attention. I recall these supernatural encounters, with humility and reverence to Him. One such encounter involved a clear instruction to pray over a bottle that was three-quarters full of olive oil, which led to my commitment in praying for a friend.

Prayer has always been an important part of my life and my usual practice was to pray early each morning. During one of my prayer sessions, I had an interesting experience that shocked me at the time. It was a clear and distinct voice calling my name. "Almina, pray over the bottle of olive oil in your cupboard, and I will cause it to rise to the top until it bubbles and spills over." Questions started flooding my mind. "Did I hear right or was that my imagination?" Fearing it was my imagination playing tricks on me, I decided not to respond, as I couldn't recall having any olive oil in the house.

During the course of the day, I pondered about what I had heard and shared the incident with my then prayer partner. She was just as surprised as me and eager to learn what it was all about. I wasn't sure what it meant and tried to put it at the back of my mind, fearing it was my imagination. However, as I spent time in prayer the following morning, I again heard the same voice. This time, I took note of the unexpected command and hurried to the kitchen to see if there was really olive oil there, as I couldn't recall purchasing any. To my amazement, the oil was in my cupboard. One of my friends was moving house and had given us the oil, along with many other items, and it had escaped my attention, as my sister did the packing.

Without hesitation, I took the oil to the front room and prayed over it and, just as the voice had said, the oil in the bottle, which was about three-quarters full, slowly rose to the top. With a bubbling noise it spilled over on the table. Overcome with excitement, I ran out of the house to call my prayer partner, and she hurriedly returned and witnessed this amazing miracle first-hand. The instruction was to go to the hospital and use the oil to anoint my friend. This we did and, along with the prayers of the church and the doctors' intervention, God healed the young lady, who today is well and continues to be a part of our church. Since that amazing experience, I developed a greater passion for praying for the sick and vulnerable and used every opportunity I had to minister to people's hurts. Today I am still involved in this area of ministry and I am convinced that that was one of God's ways of directing me to my destiny.

As the years rolled by, my life slowly changed for the better. Although I had many setbacks, things seemed to be falling into place and there was a sense of optimism in the air. I wasn't sure what was next on the horizon, but I was confident that God had bigger plans for me than I had for myself. Such knowledge gave me a strange desire to take advantage of the present opportunities rather than dwell on the past.

One Sunday I was invited to a New Testament Church convention. While I was praying, I had a vision of a man coming towards me. In the vision, he walked up to me, held my hands and looked straight into my eyes. In a clear voice, I heard these words: "This is your husband." I was overtaken by surprise and after giving it time to sink in; I shared the experience with my friends and explained what I saw. Although this was an unexpected event, excitement and happiness both embraced me, leaving me on a high for the rest of the day.

Almost a year later, I was introduced to a middle-aged man named Merrick. He was polite, friendly and had a warm personality. After spending a few minutes talking, we exchanged telephone numbers and he promised to be in touch. The following day he called and we soon developed a strong friendship and talked frequently on the phone.

Weeks later, I invited him to a prayer meeting which was held at the home of one of my friends. As soon as he entered the house, my Christian friend looked at him and said, "Almina, this is your husband." I was taken aback because he didn't quite look like the person I had seen in the vision. What was incredible was the fact that this young lady had never met him before. As far as I was concerned, he was just a good friend. It took some time before I realized that this could be my prospective husband. As the reality dawned on me I realized that I could in fact be shaking hands with destiny.

Life was full of expectations as the friendship between Merrick and myself grew. He became my rock in the difficult times and he was always there ready to help in times of need. Every now and then I thought about the vision I had earlier seen and wondered whether he was in fact destined to be my husband. I also remembered what my Christian friend had said and was strangely excited about my life.

Merrick's phone calls and visits became more frequent and as time went by, his interest in me grew. It was an interesting time for both of us as we got to know each other a little better. One day, he visited me and I was pleasantly surprised when he asked me to be his wife, with a beautiful engagement ring. Needless to say, the answer was "Yes." As he shook my hand to leave, I realized then that I was in fact shaking hands with destiny.

CHAPTER FOURTEEN
Plans for Marriage

After about two and a half years of friendship, Merrick and I decided to get married. It was exciting, but also scary. Although deep down I believe that I had made the right decision, I still had doubts. Different questions began whizzing around in my head and it was hard to control them. *What if he wasn't the right person?* I thought. *Suppose I am making a big mistake, what do I do then?* All sorts of thoughts raced through my mind as I contemplated the prospect of being a wife. I was twenty-nine years old and Merrick was forty-nine. The age gap was a bit worrying, but I gradually managed to get over that, with time.

I wanted to be sure I was doing the right thing. In order to seek guidance, I went to the principal of the college and told him about our plans for marriage. He was supportive and openly shared some of his marriage experiences, which we found helpful. After talking to us for a while he gave us his blessing for our future together.

He and his wife was a well-respected couple and we were pleased when they offered some help and advice, which came in handy for us. We met them on a few occasions and it was always encouraging to listen to their story of love and devotion. Their experience gave us hope as we looked forward to a successful marriage. Although Merrick and I were excited about our future together, we were both nervous.

I told Sandra and Charlene about our impending marriage. They were my two closest friends, whose opinions I valued very much. They were excited for me, as they had met Merrick before on a few occasions. I was happy that Merrick received their approval. I told my uncle, his wife and the other family members, who also shared my excitement. God had been faithful in putting the right people in my path. My immediate family from Jamaica also supported me in my decision and reassured me of their prayers.

After making the decision, I spent many days praying to God for guidance. It was such a big step and I wanted to be certain that this was what God wanted for us. Over the years, life had been hard enough and I didn't want to take on something that would bring me more unhappiness.

The rest of my family and friends were told about our intentions. Some questioned my choice of partner, while most accepted Merrick. As the days rolled into weeks, I became more relaxed about Merrick being my husband. He was quiet, kind and soft-spoken and he treated me with love and respect. We spent many days talking, praying and making plans for our big day.

I was almost at the end of my studies at Springdale College, and although I was looking forward to our wedding, I was concerned about the financial aspect of it. I had only been in England for a short time, and most of that time was spent studying. I had never really worked, except for doing a few odd jobs like cleaning and babysitting for relatives and friends, therefore it was difficult to contribute to the wedding. The simple fact was I didn't have a lot of money.

I discussed this with Merrick and he insisted that he would like a large church wedding. This was what I wanted too, but practically and financially, it was impossible. After much discussion, we finally settled for a registry office wedding with a few friends and relatives.

Our wedding was planned for July 30, 1988. The preparation process was both difficult and exhausting. Merrick was made redundant from his job, which created a greater financial strain on both of us, and I felt awful not being able to contribute a lot towards our wedding. However, we spent much time praying that God would meet our needs and help us through the arrangements.

We prepared the invitations, bought the rings and went in search for the dress. Our church was supportive and helpful, and they contributed financially and offered their time and energy. God had been faithful to us and we will never forget the generosity of our brothers and sisters in Christ. God faithfully supplied all our needs for our wedding, and He had again proven to us that He is a present help in times of trouble.

The principal and his wife kindly allowed us to use their cottage for the reception and contributed most of the food. My uncle and his wife donated the main cake, and my cousins from Leicester supplied the rice and chicken. Mr. and Mrs. Owens, whom we called our surrogate mother and father, also generously donated cakes as gifts. They had always been a wonderful couple and a tower of strength to us. Sonia Lawrence and Duncan Moore were the photographers for the day, and this was provided free of cost. Drinks, salad and dessert were all part of people's contributions. Thank God for a miracle we did not expect!

The day of the wedding arrived and we were both nervous. Merrick and I met at the Registry Office along with our guests, all immaculately dressed and in very high spirits. Although I was excited, I was anxious and afraid that something might go wrong.

The service was short but meaningful. We had a wonderful day and the reception was equally as good. The food, speeches, support and encouragement made the day very memorable for us. Today, we look back with sincere gratitude at the generosity of all our friends and relatives who supported us at this very special occasion in our lives.

CHAPTER FIFTEEN
Settling In as Husband and Wife

Our marriage started well and we were happy. Merrick was caring and supportive and we spent a lot of quality time with each other. We went out together and we shared in the household chores. Life was pleasant for both of us and we looked forward to better days. Merrick got a job as a machinist and I got a job in an Anglican Church working with young people and adults. It was a rewarding experience starting my first job in England. Working at the Anglican Church was interesting and the people were lovely. Things were falling into place and our dream of purchasing a house was now in sight.

We were extremely happy as we made the necessary preparations to start our life together. After what seemed like a long time, we finally moved into our new home. This was like a dream come true, and there seemed to be rays of light shining in our direction.

A few weeks after settling into our home, we were greeted with a pleasant surprise. As I was doing the ironing upstairs the door knocked, and in walked a young lady from London who was interested in looking at our property. She politely introduced herself and explained that she had recently bought a house on our road and was living a few doors away. She said that whilst house hunting, our house was her first choice but was told it had already been purchased. She was curious to see what it was like, so she knocked our door to meet us and also have a look at our home. We gave her a tour of our house, and very soon, Merrick and I were at her house looking around and going through the family album. We talked about our marriage and she shared her dreams and aspirations with us. It was interesting spending time together and getting to know each other.

It was also a big transition for her as she had recently lost her mother and had moved to Birmingham from London to continue her studies at the university. She was determined to make the best of her new environment. Not only was she pleasant and polite but also she was fun to be around. She was ambitious, giving and caring and we welcomed her with open arms. Her name was Gillian Ramsey. She became a part of our family and has been there for us through the good and bad times. We believe that God had sent her into our lives at a very crucial time and she was far more than what we expected from a friend. Merrick and I continued to be positive about our relationship, although at times, it was proving to be more difficult than what we had earlier thought.

After the first few months however, things started getting a bit shaky. We were having frequent quarrels about very simple things, and it was apparent how different we were. I was becoming unhappy, as I thought that things would only get better. Although we were compatible in many ways, it was clear that we had different ideas of doing things. This was presenting very serious problems with our relationship. Merrick was forty-nine, set in his ways and had enjoyed bachelorhood for a long time.

He was quiet and reserved and was not used to expressing his feelings. On the other hand, I was twenty-nine and had never been in a serious relationship before. I had very strong views about certain things, and I would communicate my feelings if something seemed wrong. Merrick found it challenging and threatening, and would isolate himself rather than deal with issues.

There was great friction between us about minor and trivial things, like how the toothpaste was squeezed and how his clothes were ironed. At times, he was stubborn and could not see any form of reasoning. He would frequently retreat to the spare bedroom to avoid any form of confrontation. The husband I thought I knew seemed to have disappeared.

Here I was, living on the brink of despair with a marriage that was slowly failing. I wasn't sure where the relationship was heading and I began to ask myself many questions. What about the vision I had seen? Could I have possibly made a serious mistake? I couldn't understand why those trivial things were pushing us apart and things didn't seem to be getting better. In fact, the strain from our marriage was beginning to take its toll on both of us.

Our personalities always clashed and we would occasionally end up in screaming matches to get our views across. I wasn't any angel, but I always challenged any form of negative behavior, and this created more tension between us. Our biggest problem was ironing. Merrick was used to ironing his clothes almost immediately after they were washed, and I would iron a few pieces of clothing at a time. I was expected to wash the clothes on Fridays and iron on Saturdays. As time went by, Merrick slowly disengaged himself from many of the activities in the home, leaving me to cook, do the shopping and make sure that his meals were on the table. No amount of reasoning could change his mind. Nothing less would do for him.

Merrick was still a lovely man, who tried his best to provide for the family, but he was struggling to cope with the marriage. One of our problems was communication, and I found it extremely difficult to live with a man who, at times, wasn't able to compromise. He certainly had specific expectations from me as a wife, which I wasn't sure, were workable. His idea of having a wife appeared to be, that the woman should look after the man even if both are working. The woman's responsibility was to make sure that his food is on the table, clothes are washed and ironed, shopping is done and the house is kept clean. This I detested strongly, often telling him that God did not make him with fins, instead He made him with hands and feet so that he can help with the different chores around the house. I was beginning to have doubts about our relationship, and I questioned whether I had done the right thing. Married life was getting extremely difficult.

On the good days, we spent much time discussing how to resolve our conflicts but, at times, we failed miserably because of our different personalities. We both received a lot of pleasure from each other's company, but the constant arguments placed a great strain on our relationship.

About six months into the marriage, Merrick and I had a slight disagreement and, as we were trying to discuss the problem, Merrick walked out of the house and slammed the door. He didn't return until late. This was his usual way of dealing with problems. If things were not in his favor, he would walk away to avoid dealing with it.

I challenged him regarding his behavior when he returned. I explained that if he really wanted the marriage to be a success, there was no option but to work hard at it. "Walking away was a coward's approach; boys run away but men stand up and face the challenges of life," I told him. By this time, Merrick was extremely angry, and not open to reasoning. He seemed adamant that he wasn't prepared to change. The man I knew during courtship had changed for the worse.

Angrily, he looked at me and raised his voice. The next words I heard shocked me: "You want a divorce, you want a divorce?" I couldn't believe what I heard. I could feel my blood boiling as intense rage and anger crossed my path.

I blurted out, "My God, it seems as if I am married to a coward. If you want a divorce, let's go for it, because anything else is better than this. Is that what you want, Mr. Francis? Is that what you really want?"

Having heard me so determined, he sat down, looking very reflective. I continued my conversation. "Merrick, if you really want a divorce, do the honorable thing and walk away, because I'm not prepared to come after you."

After a long pause, Merrick finally built up the courage to speak. "I don't want a divorce, I want you. I really want our marriage to work but I am not sure how this will happen." Those words almost lifted me off my feet as I shuddered with excitement. It was as if I was in a trance and suddenly came to my senses.

For the first time in a long while, we went into the front room and chatted at length about the way forward. We drafted up a plan of action on how to deal with issues affecting us, and discussed our expectations in terms of our marriage. We implemented a system of evaluating and rating our marriage on a monthly basis in terms of percentage. At that time, our marriage was only twenty percent in terms of how well we were doing as a couple.

There was hope. We loved each other and wanted our marriage to work. Our immediate plan of action included the following:

Always pray together.

Don't take each other for granted.

Always show appreciation to each other.

Say Thank you, Please, I'm sorry.

Say how you feel if you are not happy about things.

Never let the sun go down on your wrath.

Share the household chores.

This was the beginning of our long journey to a successful marriage. There had been ups and downs, but there was improvement in our relationship and things were slowly getting better. We had disagreements but they were handled much better. Instead of walking away, Merrick and I spent time having discussions, which were positive and beneficial.

Over the next few months, things began to take shape and I felt I was slowly getting my husband back and we were much happier. The process was very slow and sometimes painful, but we were determined to make our marriage work. We spent much time praying and asking God's blessing on our relationship. Bible reading was regular, and married life was becoming more pleasurable.

Some time later, I revisited the picture of Merrick, which resembled the one I had seen in the vision, and gave God thanks for bringing us together. This was an important time for us as we were now able to celebrate a happy relationship. By now, things had improved remarkably and we were now not only husband and wife, but also great friends. I realized then that a marriage will only succeed when the people involved are prepared to work hard at it.

The next few months had seen very important changes in our lives. We were now shopping together, going for short walks and enjoying each other's company. We talked about visiting Jamaica to meet the rest of the family and we made big plans for the future. There was happiness and laughter in our home and we were learning to communicate effectively again. This was an incredible journey that we didn't want to end and as time went by, things steadily improved for the better.

Life seemed more meaningful and worthwhile and there was a sense of accomplishment in our relationship. Now that things had improved, Merrick and I felt it necessary to visit Jamaica to meet the extended family, however this was not possible at the moment, as we didn't have enough money. We were both disappointed, but we decided to save for our holiday. This would give Merrick an opportunity to meet my parents and other members of my family. We were pleased however, to learn that my cousin was planning to visit England and spend some time with us. The thought of her coming was exciting and we looked forward to seeing her.

As we made the necessary preparations, memories of my rape ordeal flashed in my mind. For years, I had carried the pain around, hoping and wishing that I would have the courage to tell my cousin exactly what happened. This was perhaps going to be my opportunity. Even though I hadn't mentioned the attack in a while there were still times when it troubled my mind.

Although my cousin and I had a close relationship, we'd never really discussed intimate issues relating to our lives. At the time, she was interested in finding out what had happened but I didn't have the courage to tell her. Different thoughts raced through my mind and a surge of anger rushed through my body as I remembered the gross injustice I had faced as a child. It was important for me to express those feelings with my husband who was not only supportive but patient and understanding.

For some reason, I was determined to reveal the truth about my experience to my cousin, if the topic was revisited. Weeks later, she arrived in Birmingham and we were happy to see each other and catch up on events in our lives. She was introduced to Merrick and they got on well. We spent a lot of time chatting and sharing our experiences with each other, which was very interesting. There was no question about my abuse and deep inside I thought she had forgotten about it, so I slowly settled into the idea that this topic was never going to come up.

After going for a short walk one Saturday, we returned home and settled down to relax and watch television. The evening was bright and rays of sunlight filtered through the curtain as we exchanged conversations with each other. Merrick felt comfortable with my cousin and eagerly shared some of his experiences both in England and Jamaica. After having our meal that day, the question about my abuse came up. Although I was hoping that she remembered the events regarding my ordeal, I still felt shocked and embarrassed about going into the details. Looking straight into my eyes, my cousin asked, "Miney, do you remember the night when we went shopping and you disappeared, what really happened? Did something happen to you that night?"

Somehow, I felt like I was floating in my seat from the rush of intense apprehension and anxiety. For a brief moment, I was at a loss as to what to say and caught myself staring blankly at the wall. I swallowed my spit hard trying to build up the courage to open my mouth, as I felt dumbfounded. Where do I begin? I thought. As I tried hard to conceal the tears welling up in my eyes, I quietly made a pledge to myself. This time I will tell all.

That was exactly what I did. Although it took me a while to get started, I carefully revealed every detail of my ordeal and the name of the individual who molested me. I wasn't afraid anymore and I was determined to clear my name of any wrongdoing. As I spoke, a sense of liberation flooded my being and I felt as if I was slowly being unwrapped from the bondage that had bound me for so many years. I felt like a butterfly that had suddenly learnt that it could open its wings and fly.

Since the incident, that was the first time I had been able to share it with any of my family members and it was truly a therapeutic experience. We chatted for a long while and I was able to express the humiliation, pain and heartache I endured over the years. I also took the opportunity to address some of the rumors and gossip that had been floating around in my community.

My cousin looked numb with shock as she shared her disappointment and anger at the whole situation. Somehow, something had been released in me and I felt a sudden urge to return to my community and not only reveal the truth but also to confront my abuser and challenge the people who had treated me unjustly. I desperately wanted to bury the ghost that had haunted me for so many years.

After my cousin left, Merrick and I spent time talking about the experience gained from her and how positive it had been. We talked freely about the abuse and the effect that it had on our relationship and how we could take steps to make things better. I also told Merrick of my desire to return to Jamaica to sort out the mess that I had left behind and also to confront my molester.

Merrick wasn't sure it was a good idea so both of us prayed and handed this sorry affair to God. As I expressed my hurts and pains to Him, I was surprised at what I was experiencing. Instead of feeling the intense hatred I had experienced before, I began to feel pity for this man who had almost destroyed my life. God was taking me on the difficult road of forgiveness and for some strange reason I didn't resist Him. In the past, I had done everything except truly forgive him. Since that time, God began to teach me that in order to truly move on with my life, I needed to forgive him.

This was the way forward. Forgiveness was a process I had to go through, even though it was the hardest thing to do. Not only did I take positive steps to try and forgive my abuser, but Merrick and I also asked for forgiveness for the things we had done to each other. It was an important time for us, as God was not just healing our marriage; he was also healing our minds. The road to complete forgiveness was a long and painful journey and I often fell back into old habits of hatred, but I was willing to stay on that road until I had learnt the secret of forgiveness. The peace that I was experiencing was now too precious to leave behind. Now that a few of our issues had been dealt with, we were only just beginning to settle in as husband and wife.

CHAPTER SIXTEEN
An Uncertain Pregnancy

Our relationship had improved tremendously and Merrick and I discussed the possibility of having a baby. We told our friend Gillian Ramsey of our desire and she shared in our happiness. We were both excited about the prospect of having an extension to our family. I came from a family of nine and Merrick was from a family of three boys. We talked about having either three or four children as soon as possible, as both of us were getting on in years.

In July 1989, I became pregnant and we were overjoyed that we had been blessed to have a child. Merrick and I couldn't wait to tell our friends, who were very happy for us. Gillian stood by us every step of the way, doing everything to make our lives as comfortable as possible. She took us shopping and helped us to make the necessary preparations for our new arrival. We started making plans for our newborn baby, and we gave God thanks for the ability to conceive. It was a great day for celebration. After everything that had happened in my life, this was great cause for rejoicing.

The pregnancy started well but, as time went by, it became very difficult and I was sick most of the time, vomiting and suffering from severe pains. Earlier on in the year, I was diagnosed with large fibroids in my womb, which were making things difficult. There was continuous pain and many trips to the hospital. The doctor felt that the baby was at risk, as it was struggling for space in the womb. As the pregnancy developed, so did the fibroids. Merrick was nearly fifty years old, I was nearly thirty, and we were now in doubt as to whether our baby would survive. It was an uncertain time for both of us.

Merrick and I prayed continuously that God would look after our baby. According to the doctors, the baby was developing fine and had a good chance of survival, but was fighting for space as the fibroids increased in size. As the baby grew in my womb, I would talk and sing to it and willed it to fight for its survival. Although the future looked grim and our faith had again been shaken, we never gave up on God's ability to see us through this unpleasant time.

While my husband was at work, many hours were spent on my knees in praise and thanksgiving for this miracle that was growing in my womb. Singing became my new hobby, and I built a relationship with my child through daily communication. One of its favorite songs was "Jesus Loves Me, This I Know," and the scripture for each day was "For God so loved the world that He gave His only Son, that whosoever believes in Him should not perish but have everlasting life." The baby seemed to respond by kicking about in my womb. It was a wonderful moment for us, yet difficult at times, as the discomfort grew worse and the pains increased over the months.

A few months into the pregnancy, I woke up one night feeling unwell. The night was unsettling, as I had severe cramps in my stomach. Again, I felt as though life had chosen me for torture. All the bad things seemed to be directed towards me and I didn't know why. There are nine children in my family, yet no one else seemed to have had the constant barrage of problems I had encountered.

Neither Merrick nor I slept, as the intense pain I was experiencing kept us awake for most of the night. We weren't sure whether to call the doctor or not as I had suffered the same type of pains before. Merrick was hesitant to go to work the following day, but I reassured him that I would be fine. As was my usual practice, I went downstairs to make his sandwiches for work and we said our good-byes. My journey back upstairs was difficult, as the pain got more intense. I began to question whether I had done the right thing in encouraging Merrick to go to work.

Real panic and fear attacked me as the thought of being alone while sick plagued my mind. I managed to make it upstairs but was unable to reach the bed, as a sudden gush of blood poured from my body. I was bleeding profusely until I felt faint. I was in utter shock and disbelief. The thought of losing my baby was too much to bear.

I was confused and wasn't sure what to do or who to call, as most of my friends and relatives were at work. I looked from the bedroom window to see how far Merrick had gone but he was nowhere to be seen. I felt a sense of anger and bitterness as I was faced with yet another setback in my life. Nothing had ever been straightforward for me, I moaned. Why is life so cruel? Although I had made mistakes in the past, I tried my best to live in an appropriate way, yet life constantly dealt harshly with me. My mind went back to my youth and the hell I had been through. *When is it all going to end?* I thought.

All of a sudden, I thought about Mrs. Owens, a wonderful friend whom I call my adopted mother. She had been there for me every step of the way and had treated me just like her own daughter. As I sat soaked in blood, I dialed her number, praying that she would be at home. Thankfully, she answered the phone and rushed to my aid. Mrs. Owens made me as comfortable as possible, encouraging me to lie down until the doctor came.

Soon after, the doctor was on my doorstep. He rushed into my bedroom, examined me, and gave me the news that was my worst night-mare. "I'm sorry, Mrs. Francis, but you have lost the baby," he said.

I was devastated, as I was unable to comprehend what went wrong. I cried and asked God, "Why is this happening to me?" Why would He build up my hopes only to have them dashed to pieces? I couldn't make sense of what was happening as I found myself in a state of shock and confusion.

"My baby, my baby," I sobbed. "My beautiful baby." My heart was broken, as we wanted this baby so badly. Time was against us as we were both getting much older, and the prospect of having another child was very remote due to the fibroids. I wasn't sure what God was saying in all of this, but I had no alternative but to put everything into His hands, the one who creates life.

The ambulance was called and I was taken to the Hospital. Merrick was informed at work and met me there. He was clearly disappointed as he was looking forward to an extension to our family. His words were few as the doctors re-examined me and told me I was being kept in for observa-tion. The bleeding continued for a long time and the pains increased. The fibroids were growing rapidly and were taking their toll on my body. I was unable to eat or drink, as I vomited frequently and was feeling generally unwell most of the time.

Being in the hospital for a few days didn't calm my fears. I was still bleeding and, contrary to what my general practitioner told me, the doctors at the hospital weren't able to tell me if I had lost the baby. Days later, after speaking to the doctor, I asked whether I had miscarried, and his simple answer was, "I don't know. We'll have to wait and see if the bleeding stops. Once it stops, then we'll be able to do a scan, which will show if your baby is still alive." I was in a place of disappointment and grief, and in my turmoil, I prayed to God for help.

Quietly and prayerfully, I asked God for strength and courage, as again I found myself in the valley. I said, "Dear God, if you would allow this child to live, I promise I would give it back to you." This was out of sheer desperation and whether I seriously meant it, I'm not quite sure. All I knew was that I desperately wanted my baby. I now realize the danger of making promises to God, which I am not sure I can fulfill.

Hopelessness and despair became my acquaintances as I tried to make sense of what was happening to me. I was carrying a baby who could possibly be dead in my womb, yet I didn't know for sure. Days seemed to turn into weeks, and I was nowhere nearer the truth. The bleeding continued, and many trips to and from the hospital left me tired and drained. I cannot quite recall when the bleeding finally stopped, but it was a traumatic experience. Thankfully, I was then ready for a scan. I held my breath as I waited for the results and prayed quietly for God to breathe upon my child.

The scan showed that our baby was alive and developing well. Merrick and I were overjoyed, along with all our friends and relatives. We give all the glory and thanks to God for working a miracle for us.

Almina in England

Tamara two years old

School where Almina taught in Jamaica

Church Almina attended in Jamaica

Merrick and Almina on their wedding day

Tamara and Dad

Almina's sister Kathleen

Tamara's cousin Keiron

Tamara on her eighth birthday

Almina's niece, Sandra Edwards, who helped care for Tamara

CHAPTER SEVENTEEN
A Baby Called Tamara

A beautiful baby girl was born on the first of March 1990 by Cesarean section. She weighed in at six pounds and five ounces and she looked a picture of health, except for her bulgy stomach, which the doctor said was quite normal for a baby. She was adorable and lively, and we were grateful to God for such a wonderful gift. Merrick was overjoyed at seeing his beautiful daughter, and he gave thanks to God, who is able to perform miracles.

At the hospital she was measured, assessed and given a clean bill of health. We named her Tamara because we loved the name. After a few days at the hospital, we took her home and she appeared well, except for the frequent high temperatures that kept occurring. When this was reported to the doctors, we were told she was all right, but if it happened again, we should give her Calpol to reduce the fever.

Everyone loved Tamara, as she was such a cute baby. She was our pride and joy and meant everything to us. With all the difficulties during the pregnancy, we realized that God had brought her into the world for a purpose. What it was, we weren't very sure, but we committed her to Him who is able to direct her path.

A few months later, Tamara was dedicated at the Anglican Church where the family attended. It was a joyous occasion, as our friends and relatives came to celebrate the birth of our beautiful baby. Later in the evening, we had a party, with lively music and delicious food, and we partied the night away with a sense of gratitude to God for the gift of life. We prayed and gave thanks for the most beautiful gift of all, TAMARA FRANCIS.

Time seems to have flown by since our baby was born. At the age of two, she was communicating, running around and recognizing letters and pictures from her book, but she was an extraordinarily quiet child. She was daddy's girl, and he was very proud of her and took her almost everywhere he went. Tamara got all the attention a little girl could possibly need. Her godparents took it in turns to take her out, and lavished her with beautiful gifts. She was loved, not only by us, her parents, but also by the church, which embraced her with the love of God. We felt blessed and privileged to be her parents, and each day we reminded her how special and unique she was.

We later made preparations for a visit to Jamaica to introduce Tamara to our family, but because of lack of finance, Merrick was unable to accompany us. Although he was clearly disappointed, he decided that Tamara and I should go until we had a chance to visit as a family. Tamara's grandfather was in his eighties, grandmother was in her sixties, and it was important for her to meet her extended family. The night before our flight, Tamara became ill with severe diarrhea, vomiting and an extremely high temperature. She looked tired and weak and it was a worrying time for us. We called the doctor to explain our concerns and stressed how sick she was. We also wanted some reassurance on whether to travel or not. We were willing to call off the travel arrangements until Tamara was well enough, but the doctor assured us she would be fine. We gave her the remedies suggested and the illness slightly calmed down.

We went to Jamaica in March 1992 and had a brilliant time, although the vomiting and diarrhea persisted for a couple of weeks. Tamara met numerous members of the family and she was not short of places to go. Everyone embraced her lovingly and it didn't take long before she felt at home among the family. We had many tours, visited friends we had met in England and, as usual, I was invited to a few churches to preach. We arrived back in England after a wonderful holiday in Jamaica. God had been faithful and kept our daughter well on our holiday, and we were grateful for His protection.

CHAPTER EIGHTEEN
An Extraordinary Vision Revealed

As time went by, God continued to heal our relationship and we learnt to appreciate the blessings that He had bestowed upon us. Our greatest blessing was our beautiful daughter that He had given us and each day we gave thanks for the joy that she had brought to our lives. Merrick and I had regular Bible Studies and discussions and we spent a lot of time communicating about different issues that affected us. This was truly a liberating time for us. There was joy and peace in our home, which had made a huge difference to our lives.

I felt like the broken pieces of my life were in the process of being restored. Something extraordinary appeared to be on the verge of taking place. I was learning to love myself in a fresh way and my confidence was slowly coming back. I couldn't help feeling like I was on the brink of a new beginning. The smell of anticipation littered the air like a sweet fragrance and a deep passion for clarity about my background erupted within me like a volcano. My crave for clarity became greater than my drive for change. Somehow, I needed to be clear about my past in order to make changes for the future. I didn't want anything to stop me from being the best mother to my daughter. She was my main priority now, therefore it was imperative that I didn't make the same mistakes that my parents had made.

I knew that this process wasn't going to be easy but I was prepared to take one step at a time, until I arrived at a place of purpose and inner peace. It was during this period that I was introduced to a young lady called Yvonne Arthurs. She was a committed Christian who was enthusiastic about her faith. As the friendship grew, she shared some of her experiences, which helped to clarify some of my past issues. Not only did we engage in prayer and Bible Studies, but we also spent a lot of time talking. I no longer felt alone. There was somebody else I could share with, regarding my experience of marriage, loneliness and abuse.

Yvonne had interesting dreams that were always timely and significant and I had wonderful experiences of closeness to God, as he revealed things through prayer, which were also fascinating. Being able to share with someone who understands was very liberating. In a strange way I felt that God was directing my steps and enabling me to confront my past.

Being at the Anglican Church was rewarding for our family. It was wonderful venturing out into something new. It gave us a fresh understanding of a different style of worship that we found interesting and enjoyable. However, due to the new addition to our family and the distance church was away from home, it became difficult to make regular trips to the meetings. Because of this, Merrick and I felt it was time to look for a new Church.

In order for us to make important decisions about our lives, our usual practice was to pray and seek God's guidance. This was always our first point of reference. As we prayed, I had an amazing experience. It was like watching myself on a television screen. Very clearly, I saw myself standing on a pulpit preaching to a congregation of people and heard a distinct voice saying, "Go to Beacon Church and minister to my people." Without hesitation, I discussed this with my husband, who also confirmed his desire to be a member of Beacon Evangelical Church. That experience left me feeling like, at long last I was finally going to a Church where our family would settle indefinitely.

We were no strangers to Beacon church, as we had visited a few times. The people were lovely and supportive and it didn't take long for us to feel a sense of belonging there. Whilst visiting Beacon, a group called the Monday Fellowship was formed and we met weekly for Bible Studies and prayer and also to encourage each other. This gave us a platform to share our experiences both openly and honestly. The meetings were empowering, as each person shared their stories of triumph in the midst of adversity. I began to realize that my experiences—although negative—were a stepping-stone to bigger and greater things to come.

As time went by, I slowly learned to praise God through my circumstances and He gave me a bigger platform to share His word. Sharing my experience was very therapeutic and this created the opportunity to meet other people with similar experiences. This further enhanced the healing process in my life.

About one year later, I received the right hand of fellowship and became a member of Beacon Church and soon after I was elected as a deacon. During that time, I received many invitations to speak at different churches. Through my testimonies, I was able to expose my wounds, in the hope that at least one person who had suffered in silence over the years, would somehow find the strength and courage to deal with their trauma. This I did with much fervor and enthusiasm and God blessed my ministry.

My life was now taking a new shape, as the pains of my past had become a source of healing for people's hurt and despondency. God was not only opening doors for ministry, but He was unraveling the mysteries of my trauma and putting me in touch with my destiny. Beacon Church had been a stepping-stone to greater things in my life. The Monday Fellowship became a source of encouragement and God opened many avenues for new friendships and ministries. His purposes for my life were slowly being revealed and life seemed more meaningful as the process of inner healing continued to take place.

It was clear God had handpicked various people to minister to my hurts and also to bring joy and laughter into my life. Gillian James brought that sense of fragrance to the fellowship, with her contagious sense of humor and her charming personality. Her wild laughter was like an antidote for open wounds and her frequent tears while praising God was refreshing and uplifting. It is true that laughter is like a good dose of medicine for the soul, because it replenishes the inner man with gladness. Laughter reaches the place where neither tablets nor medicine can reach, and it helps in the healing process of our lives. It is in those times that I became more conscious of God's desire to heal my mind so that I could truly embrace myself again.

It was encouraging to see the bond and the level of friendship that existed amongst us. There was the feeling of genuine love, sincerity and honesty and everyone looked out for each other. As I enjoyed the new friendships and shared in discussions, I was conscious that although things seemed to be going well and there was obvious progress in my life, I still had a long way to go for complete healing and restoration to take place.

This phase of my life had been reflective and empowering and it gave me a buzz to be the best I could be in every way possible. Being the best mother and wife meant I was succeeding in one of life's greatest experiences. I wanted to offer Tamara the best of what I never had. Even though I would have liked to offer her a small measure of riches and prosperity, I would still have chosen the greatest gifts that a child can have, which is love, peace and security. On these hang success and fulfillment. These cannot be bought with money or earthly possessions. They are the rights of children and they deserve it. I am painfully aware that childhood scars can very often leave a dent in people's character, which can linger for a long time if it's left untreated.

Life's journey can be difficult, and at times the road seemed to be paved with the feelings of highs and lows, positives and negatives, mountaintop and valley experiences and there is always the sense that we are on the verge of something new. Things do not appear to remain stationary for a long time. There is always movement that seems to determine our state of mind from one day to the next. For some people, happiness is like a fleeting gesture while sadness has become a permanent stalker for others. However difficult life gets, I am determined to try and appreciate the good moments and pray that God will teach me to deal with the bad. Although things hadn't been easy at times, my experience as a wife, mother and fellowship leader had taught me more about myself than I had learnt in a long time.

My operation date had finally arrived and I was eager to get it over with. After what seemed like a long wait, I underwent a major operation to remove the fibroids I had during pregnancy. My sister came from Jamaica to help care for Tamara. Her support at a time when we needed it most had helped me to make a quick recovery.

During this period, Tamara continued to have a high temperature, which her doctor was aware of. He reassured us that she was fine, but we decided to watch her progress, as things didn't seem right. The Monday Fellowship group was growing in number and they prayed for Tamara constantly. The meetings were always vibrant and we felt encouraged and supported by the members.

At three years old Tamara was enrolled in nursery. She was bright but extremely quiet. Earlier on, I took her to the doctor to find out if her quietness was due to any medical problems. According to the doctor, she was fine.

Apart from the frequent high temperature and the distorted-looking tummy, she appeared well, but the frequency of her illness gave us cause for concern. She enjoyed going out, loved singing and dancing, and was an adorable child who was never a problem. She learnt to pray at an early age and often joined in prayer with the family.

One night as I knelt down at my bedside to pray, I had one of the most unusual experiences that was to change the course of my life. To this day, I cannot forget the date: December 12, 1993. During prayer, I had a vision about Tamara. It was like watching a movie on a television screen. I wasn't asleep; I was fully aware of my environment. In the vision, I saw a coffin that had rolled down from the top of a hill. When it came to a standstill, I was shocked and disturbed by it. Then I heard a voice commanding me to go over to the coffin. I was hesitant at first, but then I willed myself to go. It was as if I was being lifted out of my body, and I saw myself very clearly walking over to the coffin.

As I got there, the lid flipped open and, to my utter amazement, I saw my daughter lying there. She appeared to be either dead or in a coma. She was dressed in white and her eyes were closed. Her hands were by her side and there was no movement at all.

I stood over the coffin trembling and shaking, not knowing what to do. Then I heard another voice saying, "Tell Tamara to arise and come forth." In response to the command, I raised my voice and said, "Tamara, arise and come forth." At the sound of my voice, her eyes opened and she sat up. She then got out of the coffin and came towards me. She held my hand and as we walked away, I looked down and noticed, to my surprise, she was much older than she actually was. I was stunned and began to mutter to myself, "What is happening here? This child looks much older than she really is." "For heaven's sake, she is only three years old."

Then I heard another voice saying, "When Tamara gets older, she will be sick to the point of death, but God will restore her health." I began to ignore the vision, hoping it would go away, but it was very clear to me that it had to come to pass.

The vision ended but I was extremely concerned. I was frightened of losing my only daughter, and very sad that this nightmare was hanging over our heads. It was like a death sentence that I could do nothing about. That same night, I shared my experience with my husband, who was also disturbed by it. I found it difficult to sleep as I tried to make sense of what I had just seen. Visions weren't new to me; they had always been a part of my life since my youth, but to have a vision of my own child was beyond words. Out of desperation and great concern I also shared my experience with members of the Monday Group, people from my church, and many of my family and friends.

CHAPTER NINETEEN
The Unfolding of the Vision

Two years after the vision, Tamara's health began to deteriorate. There were frequent trips to the doctors, as different changes began to take place in her body. Her eyes became yellow and no one seemed to know the real reason. She was sick almost every two weeks, with an extremely high temperature and she was unable to move. Anyone who witnessed her illness was fearful that she might die, yet the doctors kept reassuring us that she was fine.

She was referred to the City Hospital, where she was given a clean bill of health. As a mother, I knew that she was ill and no one could convince me otherwise. Tamara's tummy was so large it was obvious that something was wrong with her. Most of my friends knew she was sick, just by looking at her, yet the only people who didn't seem to know were the doctors. The illness was so rare that they didn't even suspect that anything was wrong.

Months later Tamara's condition worsened and again I took her to the doctor. After the consultation, I was left feeling that I was neglecting my daughter. I explained the symptoms and stressed how unwell she had been; however, the doctor didn't take much notice. He remained adamant that there was nothing wrong with her. Instead, he went on to ask questions about our lifestyle, which left me feeling distressed and unhappy. One didn't need a medical book to see Tamara was ill. A little more investigation would have been welcomed.

Another two years went by and we were no nearer to the truth about Tamara's illness. She was attending Rookery Junior School but her attendance was erratic at times due to poor health. Since birth, she had been plagued with frequent high temperature and constant abdominal pains. Her stomach was always distorted, and gradually her eyes became jaundiced. Despite this, no one detected how ill she actually was. Out of desperation, I spoke to different doctors. I also discussed her problems with both the school nurse and doctor and, to my dismay; everyone seemed to think that she was fine.

After many journeys to the doctor, Tamara was again referred to City Hospital. It was obvious that her health was deteriorating rapidly and the illness was invading her small body, as other frightening changes took place. Having exhausted all the avenues available to us, Merrick and I prayed and committed our daughter to God for His safekeeping. He was the only one we could put our total trust in, and we were confident that God would see us through this difficult time, as He had a purpose for her life.

At the hospital, a doctor examined her and to my horror, he looked at me, nodded his head and said, "Mrs. Francis, your daughter is seriously ill. She needs to be referred immediately to the Children's Hospital. I will make the referral but I need to talk with both you and your husband, as this is very serious."

I rushed home in a taxi with Tamara and told my husband all about my ordeal at the hospital. We were both relieved that at least a diagnosis would finally be made yet, at the same time, anxious and nervous about the possible implications for our daughter.

My heart broke as I began to review the different chapters of my life. Almost every page was lined with misadventures and insurmountable pain that somehow seemed too unfair for words. Since Tamara was one year old, Merrick and I desperately tried for another child. We pursued different avenues but it never happened. Both of us received treatment at the City Hospital to improve our chance of conceiving, but it was difficult, as my fibroids had grown back.

As I reviewed my life, I couldn't believe this was happening. This was yet another obstacle in my life. However, the vision of Tamara reminded me that, in God's time, everything would be all right. That gave me great consolation and the reassurance that, whatever happened, Tamara would live. My tears flowed freely as I thought about Tamara's future.

Just then, the phone rang. It was the doctor from City Hospital, who had earlier examined Tamara. "Mrs. Francis, can you and your husband make your way to the hospital? I need to speak to you immediately." Our hearts almost stopped as we listened to the urgency in his voice. We made our way to the hospital and were given the worst possible news. Tamara had a serious, rare and life-threatening liver disease, and needed to be referred to the Children's Hospital for immediate treatment. We knew she was sick, but the word 'life-threatening' nearly knocked us to the floor. Our only daughter's life was being weighed in a balance, but the vision was never far from our minds.

CHAPTER TWENTY
A Rare Illness Discovered

On December 12, 1995, Tamara was taken to the Children's Hospital and was diagnosed as having Autoimmune Chronic Hepatitis. This is a rare and incurable illness that affected about one in 100,000 children at that time. According to one doctor, difficulty in diagnosis is common and can be overlooked, sometimes for years, unless the doctor is aware of the symptoms. The illness leads to the body rejecting the liver, causing scarring and inflammation, and could possibly lead to death.

After all the years of suffering, Tamara was finally diagnosed. Her illness became a matter of urgency and gave the doctors great cause for concern. Merrick and I had to endure the trauma of being told the truth about our daughter. It was both grim and frightening, but somehow the vision had stuck in our minds. According to the doctors, her situation could lead to death, or she would need to have a liver transplant.

The thought of a liver transplant sent chills down my spine. It was difficult enough knowing that our child had a rare liver problem, but it was almost impossible to entertain the concept of a transplant. It was hard to think about somebody else's organ in my daughter's body. How on earth would that work, and what does God think about it? For months I couldn't read the newspaper or watch television programmes involving operations for fear of seeing anything to do with transplantation. I had never met anyone who had had a transplant and I wasn't sure of the long-term effects. Different questions flooded my mind, which were almost driving me into a panic attack. I became frightened and confused and was in a state of shock for a long time. This was too much for my mind to comprehend so I made a decision to leave it all in the hands of God, our Creator.

As the days went by, the vision became clearer, as the fulfillment was taking place in front of our eyes. I remembered it as if it were yesterday, and I recounted my steps back to the moment when Tamara walked away from death, in the vision. During a discussion with one of the nurses, I found the courage to share my experience with him. Although at times I didn't feel very confident, I still believed that, despite the prognosis, Tamara would survive her ordeal.

Our daughter was now registered as a patient at the Children's Hospital, where the doctors, nurses and social worker all played a vital role in her care. Their help and expertise was invaluable during this difficult period. We were supported every step of the way, and we found it a little easier to cope, due to the help and encouragement we received.

Tamara was admitted for urgent treatment. She was given large doses of steroids and about eight or ten other drugs. Her life at five years old was going through a massive transition, and she learnt the secret of praying and trusting God at an early age. Tamara went through rigorous tests, biopsies and frequent blood monitoring. At times, she was hardly able to move, as her tummy had become twice the size it used to be. She became restless and worn from the illness, yet she didn't complain. She endured her illness like a champion, always surprising us by doing the impossible. We felt very blessed to have such a special child called Tamara.

The high doses of medication were taking their toll on this young child. Her complexion darkened and many other changes took place in her small body. Large doses of steroids rapidly changed her appearance. Her small cute face became moon-shaped and her eyes were bright yellow from the jaundice. Our daughter now was hidden behind the shadow of the illness yet, in her strange-looking eyes, shone the mark of determination and a will to survive.

Days later, we were sent home from the hospital with a large supply of drugs. Although we were happy to be home, I felt a sense of unease about administering the medication to my daughter. I was afraid of giving her the wrong dosage and was worried about how the drugs might affect her. It was an extremely difficult time for us as we searched for answers to our problems. The concept of liver transplantation consumed my mind and at times almost overwhelmed me. I could not get the thoughts out of my head, and I spent many sleepless nights worrying over it. Out of fear, I continued to avoid anything relating to transplantation. I also spent many days trying to come to terms with our ordeal.

As I watched my daughter deteriorate, I became both angry and bitter. The medications weren't working as expected, and her eyes were glossy and yellow. The itching was severe and she was in constant discomfort. She was too weak to walk around and had to be lifted almost everywhere. Her body ached from diarrhea and vomiting. Tamara was suffering terribly and there was nothing we could do.

Never before had I found myself asking so many "whys." I became angry with God for allowing my daughter to endure such torment at such a young age. For a while, I refused to pray as I felt that God wasn't capable of answering my prayers. We felt as if everything was against us, but our friends and church members refused to give up. They prayed, visited and supported us in every way possible. They constantly reminded us about the vision I had about Tamara, and they were confident that God would bring her through. That gave us the courage to carry on.

Today, we owe our gratitude to all our friends, relatives and church members who supported us through the dark and eerie times. Tamara's godmother, Gillian Ramsey, stood by us every step of the way. She sacrificed her time and energy to help care for Tamara, very often taking her to her favorite places. She also took us to and from hospital in times of emergency. We owe our deepest appreciation to her. Praise be to God for His mercy and faithfulness towards us.

CHAPTER TWENTY-ONE
A Real Survivor

Tamara's illness had affected her in many ways. Her young life revolved around taking numerous medications and making regular visits to the hospital. Her immune system was weak, which caused her to be susceptible to various infections. She had good and bad days, but not once did she complain. She never grumbled about the medications or the amount she had to take repeatedly, some two or three times per day. She was an inspiration to both family and friends.

At six years old, Tamara and I jetted off to Jamaica to attend my grandmother's funeral. She was ninety-six years old when she died, and although Tamara was ill, she had recovered enough to travel. The doctor gave her the okay and we boarded the plane with a small suitcase full of medication and a letter from the doctor explaining her illness, should she fall ill in Jamaica.

We landed in Jamaica to a very warm and welcoming greeting. Everyone was delighted to see us, but very shocked to see the change in Tamara. Her eyes were bright yellow, her complexion had changed and she was now conscious of her appearance. Still she managed to smile and

126

make the best of her holiday. She became the center of attention as family and friends made a fuss of her.

It was extremely difficult for me, as I was not only mourning the loss of my grandmother, but also my uncle's wife, who died approximately one year prior to my grandmother's death. Two members of the family I had grown up with had all passed away in a matter of a few years. I was unable to attend the funerals of my uncle's wife as Tamara was extremely ill at the time, and the doctor advised me not to travel with her.

Here I was, at my grandmother's funeral, mourning her death with a daughter who could possibly face death herself. The reality of death and its finality gave me a strange determination to make the most of life, and fight for my young daughter's survival. My grandmother had enjoyed life for ninety-six years, and all her organs were intact, yet Tamara was only six years old, and her liver was seriously inflamed and scarred by a very rare liver disease. It was hard to make sense of the unfairness of life.

I missed my grandmother terribly. I remembered all the good times we had together, and I wished I could say 'thank you' once again. She had been my inspiration and a great source of strength to me.

My mind went back to when I was leaving home to settle in England. Our good-byes were tearful and it was difficult for both of us, as we had spent many years together. Grandmother seemed very unsettled and almost had a look of anger concealed in her eyes. I wasn't sure what to make of it until I went to say my final farewell. To my utter amazement, she blurted out, "Miney, I looked after you since you were a baby and I thought you would be here to take care of me, but instead you choose to leave." After saying those words she looked at me pitifully and cried for a few minutes, holding on to my hands tightly.

I nearly fell over in astonishment. To this day, I am not sure whether she really got over the shock of me leaving her and I wasn't sure whether to feel guilty or not. All those thoughts flooded my mind as I remembered life with grandmother, my uncle and his wife. These were special memories that I valued and cherished.

It was a great honor to preach at my grandmother's funeral service and to say 'thank you' to a woman who had touched my life and taught me morals and values. Her example taught me to love and help those less fortunate than myself and be considerate to all the people who come across my path.

At the end of the service, Tamara and I wept together for a grand-mother who meant so much to us. Although she had passed on, I still cherished the fond memories of her life. Life seemed empty without her and many people from the community mourned her loss and talked about how she had touched their lives.

Time seemed to have flown by quickly since the funeral and it was soon time for us to return home. I spent a few days with my cousin who had visited us in England and it was wonderful meeting again. We had many interesting times together and visited a few places of interest and also friends who lived in the same area. We talked about our grandmother and her late mother who had passed on a few years ago. We shared the memories of growing up in our community and the good and bad times that we'd had. It was a reflective time for both of us.

As I talked about my childhood, floods of memories from my abuse gushed through my mind. I could not control my thoughts, as the urge to finally do something about it became my main priority. Somehow, I felt it was imperative for me to retrace my steps to the place of the abuse and meet the man who had abused me so many years ago. Although I knew that it wasn't going to be easy, I was prepared to take the risk. I desperately wanted to tell him about the hell he had put me through. I felt he needed to know about the pain and the embarrassment I had suffered because of his actions. Somehow, it seemed necessary to confront him, so that he can at least think of the harm his behavior can have on peoples' lives. Hopefully, my conversation with him would help to protect other young and vulnerable children who may be in danger of the same fate as myself.

The fact that my grandmother had been laid to rest gave me a fresh determination to bury the ghost of my past, once and for all. I was determined not to leave Jamaica until this was resolved in order for me to make a new start. God was certainly doing something in me, as I didn't feel the intense anger and hatred that I felt before. Now I was more able to deal with the situation, and I was slowly learning to forgive him although it wasn't an easy thing to do.

His mother was a well-respected member of the community who had played a very important part in our lives as children. Most people who had immigrated to other places would visit her whilst on their vacation, with gifts, as a means of saying thank you. This was my opportunity to visit and have a chat, but more importantly, I wanted to meet her son to tell him of the hurt I had endured because of his assault. Although I desperately wanted to do this, for some reason I felt nervous and anxious and at times questioned whether I was doing the right thing. There were times when the whole situation became increasingly overwhelming, and I had no alternative but to release it to God asking Him for His wisdom.

After returning from my cousin, I decided to visit his mother with a few items I had bought for her. This was a way of expressing my appreciation for the contribution she had made to my life. Her son was still living with her, but I wasn't sure if he would be home that day. The desire to talk to him became a matter of urgency and I prayed and asked for guidance. As I reached close to their home, there he was, sitting on the wall with a broad smile over his face. "Hello, and how are you?" he said politely. All of a sudden, my heart began to race within me and bubbles of sweat began to form on my forehead. This was rather unusual as I wasn't feeling angry or fearful; instead, I was experiencing steady streaks of anxiety rushing through my body.

After collecting my thoughts, I smiled and said, " I'm fine, thank you," and before I knew it, we were talking about different things. The conversation was interesting and flowed naturally, and instead of wanting to beat this man to a pulp, I felt pity for him. Obviously, I was still distraught about the injustice I had suffered and the fact that he had robbed me of my innocence at such an early age, but I was learning to deal with it in a different way.

As we talked, different thoughts entered my mind on how to approach the subject of the rape ordeal. As we got deeper into the conversation, there seemed to be no suitable time to discuss this uncomfortable topic, and I was afraid I would miss the opportunity, so I held my breath and paused in the middle of his sentence. Before he could say another word, I nervously interrupted by asking the dreaded question, "Do you remember the time when you pulled me down those steps and what you did to me?" Without hesitating to catch my breath, I continued, " What you did hurt so badly and almost destroyed my life. To be honest, if I knew then what I know now you would be behind bars. You really made my life hell and almost ruined my reputation." As I spoke, he listened, then nodded his head and whispered what seemed to be the word, "Sorry."

He was about to say something more when his mother saw me and excitedly invited me into her house. "O God, not now, wrong timing," I murmured to myself. We both looked at each other and he slowly moved away, giving me the opportunity to respond to his mother. Not only was I uneasy with the sudden interruption but also disappointed that he was unable to further respond to my statements. For a while, I was left feeling numb with regret and disbelief. "Miney, I have been waiting to see you for a long time," his mother said welcomingly. "Since your arrival from England, we haven't had a chance to talk." By that time I was shaking, my hands were sweaty and my eyes were filled with tears at both the thought of his reaction and the incompleteness of the conversation, yet I was happy that he may have apologized for his actions. Even more important was that I had the guts to confront him. This gave me a sense of accomplishment and I felt good for it.

Even though I didn't get the desired result, I gave myself the permission to enjoy the temporary feeling of accomplishment instead of beating myself for the things that were undone. As I turned to walk away, I looked him straight in the eye and nodded my head. It was my way of saying, "Thank you for your time, but I've been through hell and high waters, I've survived and here I am."

That day, I learned the true meaning of forgiveness. It was as if a heavy weight had been lifted off my shoulders. As I slowly walked into his mother's house, I felt as if I was walking away from my chains. I was somehow leaving my past behind, never to be tortured by it again.

Nevertheless, there was something more I needed to do that day. I was determined to retrace my steps to the place where the abuse took place. Although many things in the community had changed, I just wanted to be there, for whatever reason I wasn't very sure.

After going through different emotions, I finally settled down to greet his mom. I was extremely happy to see her as she has always been a loving and generous woman. Although age had crept upon her, she continued to be a tower of strength to the community, always caring about people's well being. I didn't hold any malice or grudge against her. As far as I was concerned, she did all she could to raise her children in the best possible way.

We spent a long time chatting and catching up on the past. We talked about the passing of my grandmother, who was her good friend, and the new developments in the country. I had the opportunity of telling her about life in England and she shared with me some of the things that happened in her life. It was an interesting time. After spending about an hour with her, I kissed her goodbye and left, feeling happy that I had seen her.

On leaving her house, I asked a friend to accompany me to the shop that was a few yards away. Without further explanation, we were on our way and I was determined to use the opportunity to do what I needed to do. As I got close to the place of the abuse, I stopped and stood there for a few minutes with my mind drifting all over the place. It was like reliving every moment of my ordeal as I thought about every detail of what happened. After what seemed like minutes, I discreetly stooped down and picked up four stones, which I put in my pocket.

It was strange, because when the abuse took place I was young, powerless and naïve, and didn't have a name for what he did to me. Now, I was in control. I was no longer in the dark. I had a name for what he did to me and I wasn't afraid anymore. I could now face the fact that I had been RAPED without taking the blame. Such feeling put me in a position of having some form of control and gave me a sense of authority.

I took the stones home and after a well-deserved time of reflection, I used a red marker to write the words RAPE over them, one letter on each stone. After holding them in my hands for a few minutes, using all my energy, I threw them as far as I could and watched them disappear through the trees. This was one of the most liberating moments in my life. The simple but profound ritual meant that I was no longer under the curse of my past nor did it have any more control over my life. In fact, the experience was symbolic of me taking back my life and making a fresh start.

I was grateful that God gave me the courage to fulfill my desire. I may never know what my attacker was to say, and although I wish I knew, the whole experience was enough for me and I felt like a burden had been lifted. I give God the glory for the strength and the wisdom in helping me to deal with the difficult problems.

After putting the blame where it belonged, I was ready to face my community as a victor and not a loser. With my head held high and a spring in my steps, I was able to walk with confidence and, at times, there was the need to lovingly reprimand those who dared to point the finger of accusation towards me. For my few remaining days in Jamaica, I took the opportunity to set the record straight, by telling most of my friends and acquaintances what really happened so many years ago.

After an adventurous four weeks in the sun, with the death of my grandmother still fresh in my mind and following my confrontation with my attacker, I felt both tired and emotionally drained and was glad to return to England. We arrived back to damp weather but Tamara felt well, as the sunshine seemed to have done her some good. However, the side effects from the medication had changed her appearance even more, but she managed to get on with life.

She returned to school and some of her classmates were unable to recognize her. The teachers were informed of her progress, but her class teacher was reluctant to reintroduce her to the class, as she was not sure what to make of the changes. Not wanting Tamara to feel isolated, I briefly explained to the children that she was still the same person, but the medication had changed her appearance. The children accepted Tamara and it wasn't long before she was back to normal.

At school, she made progress in her work, although her attendance was irregular due to various hospital appointments. Most of her teachers were pleased with her work, and we were very proud of her. She joined the Perry Barr Dance School, where she did ballroom dancing. She also had piano lessons and private tuition to help her catch up with her schoolwork. She was active and was engaged in different activities. She was as special as she was extraordinary.

Tamara's will to survive was remarkable. At six years old, her incredible strength of character and determination to fight for survival has won her great admiration from both family and friends. One can only describe her as a great source of encouragement and a "real survivor."

CHAPTER TWENTY-TWO
A Turn for the Worse

Tamara was now twelve years old and growing into a beautiful young lady. She joined the youth group at her church and very quickly made friends. Although she was not well at times, she was willing to participate in various physical activities. According to one of her youth leaders, Tamara never complained. If she felt unwell, she would stop and rest. That would be the only indication that something was wrong. Tamara resented people having a pity party around her and did not want to be treated differently by her peers. Therefore, she kept her illness a secret and was very angry if people found out.

Tamara went ice-skating, rock climbing, canoeing and joined in numerous other sports that she enjoyed. On weekends, she went shopping with her friends and cycling with her cousins. Her auntie took her out to many places of interest and sometimes to our extended family in Dudley or Walsall. Tamara has always been adventurous and never liked to stay indoors. Most of her weekends were spent with family, friends and church members. She was an active child who got up early, did her homework and housework without being told, and was generally a wonderful person to be around. She had a passion for cooking and baking cakes, and during her spare time, she tried out different dishes. Anyone who loved cooking was Tamara's friend. She was not just our daughter; she was everybody else's daughter.

Starting secondary school was both exciting and scary for Tamara, and for the first time, she looked on her medication with great contempt. She was now twelve years old and her outlook on life was changing. Although she had no choice, she hated the idea of being restricted by so many different medications. Being ill for such a long time was no fun and it was beginning to affect her social life. She was at an impressionable time in her life, and it was important for her to share in the activities that her friends enjoyed; yet, life had chosen her to be different. She disliked the fact that life had been so cruel to her, and every now and then she asked, "Why me?"

Tamara's health also began to deteriorate and she started to suffer from different illnesses, and was very often unwell. It seemed as if her body had being attacked from every angle. Symptoms that we hadn't seen for years were now returning, and Tamara was riddled with pain and discomfort. Not only was it frightening for her, but also for us as parents. This often left us anxious and at our wits' end.

We frequently visited the Children's Hospital and our family doctor to seek help and advice regarding Tamara's condition. She suffered from many different complaints and she became withdrawn. Her inability to take part in some of the activities that she once enjoyed made her very sad. Those who knew her became concerned about her health as they watched her slowly deteriorate. This was one of the most trying periods for our family as we battled with grief and frustration.

Tamara was now in and out of school, her church attendance became irregular, and she was getting too weak to go out with her friends on the weekends. As she got weaker, our prayers to God increased. Often we could hear her praying for the things we take for granted. She would often cry, "Oh God, please help me to go shopping with my friends without feeling faint and unwell. Help me to walk for a few minutes without the severe pains in my feet. God, I'm scared of the muscle spasms, they hurt so much, please take it away from me. Moreover, the itching is killing me and my fingers stiffen and refuse to bend, preventing me from scratching my body. Dear God, how I wish I was a piece of stick which cannot feel any pain."

At this point, she would burst into tears and cry painfully and loudly as she told God, "I don't want to live anymore, I want to die. How I wish I was dead." Words are inadequate to express the grief and sadness we felt, as we wept for the daughter God had given us. A twelve-year-old who didn't want to live anymore—very heart-rending.

As time went by, Tamara lost all her church and school friends, except one. The friends she had met at dance school were gone, as she found it almost impossible to go out. From being a popular girl who had many friends visiting her, Tamara was now down to one friend. She was now going through what we can only describe as "hell and high waters." For what reason and purpose, we were not sure.

For eighteen months, we struggled as a family with Tamara's poor health. It was obvious that she was suffering both emotionally and physically. Very often, loud sighs were heard and her sobs became more frequent as she weighed up the enormity of her ordeal. Nothing could comfort her as she watched her body slowly failing her.

Not only was Tamara suffering from the effects of the liver disease, she was also having severe pains in her feet and frequent muscle spasms. The muscles in her arms and legs became hard at times, leaving her in excruciating pain. It was impossible for her to move and many times, she had to be helped to her bedroom. The diarrhea had increased and the jaundice in her eyes had gotten worse. There was continuous pain in her stomach, which was slowly getting bigger. She was suffering from severe itching, which continued all through the night. Because of this, parts of her body became bruised. Tamara was tortured from head to toe and all we could do was try different types of remedies, which were sometimes useless.

All the members of the family joined together to see how best they could help to alleviate some of Tamara's pain and discomfort. Her best friend, Selina, had been a tower of strength to her. She rubbed her with calamine lotion while my husband and I helped to massage her body to relieve the itching. Keiron, my nephew, brought her drinks when she needed it. He helped in whatever ways he could and never once grumbled about running different errands for us. He greatly missed Tamara's company, as she was unable to play their usual games. She was now even too weak to help him with his homework, which she enjoyed doing.

Tamara and Keiron grew up like brother and sister and had always done things together. Now that Tamara was ill, Keiron felt alone, and frequently mentioned how much he missed her. Although she was at home, she was too overwhelmed by her sickness to enter into much dialogue with anyone. There was no improvement in Tamara's condition and she continued to deteriorate.

CHAPTER TWENTY-THREE
He Who Feels It, Knows It

Tamara continued to experience severe pain and discomfort. The liver function tests were now showing more scarring and inflammation. According to her consultant, a biopsy was now necessary in order to assess the condition of the liver. Because of this, Tamara was admitted into the Children's Hospital for the biopsy. This was both worrying and stressful for Tamara. Over the years, whenever she had a biopsy, she always ended up with severe pains in her stomach for over a week. As parents, we were also anxious that Tamara would end up feeling worse after her ordeal.

Due to the pain in her feet, Tamara was barely able to walk. This was difficult for her, and she was concerned that she might end up in a wheelchair. Having to deal with this and all her other complications made it almost impossible for her to cope.

Her friend, Selina, was always there for her, supporting and encouraging her, even when she sustained a foot injury, and was away from school herself. Her doctor had advised her mother to keep her away from school until she was able to tackle the numerous stairs. In the meantime, she attended physiotherapy sessions.

Because of her commitment to her friend, she promised Tamara she would help her through her ordeal in whatever way she could. Although Selina had badly sprained her ankle and was in constant pain herself, her love for her friend became the focal point, and she continued to visit Tamara at the hospital, in an attempt to cheer her up. Her courage, consistency and dedication extended way beyond her years.

Tamara's pain and discomfort continued throughout her hospital stay. Her nights were sleepless and restless due to the intense itching and frequent visits to the toilet. The nurses were called regularly to administer painkillers for her ongoing stomach pains. Both Selina and I tried to cheer up Tamara by telling jokes and reading stories. We also prayed that God would give her a good night's rest and relief from her discomfort. Tamara managed to smile through her pain as Selina and I tried to keep her spirits up. Selina was like an antidote for Tamara as her bubbly and confident presence lifted her spirit.

It was extremely tiring as our nights were laborious and exhausting. None of us slept as our time was devoted to help bring relief to Tamara. Although Tamara was admitted into the hospital, I still felt lonely and isolated. A sense of desperation overwhelmed me as I watched her suffer physically, mentally and emotionally, without being able to do anything about it.

Tamara had the liver biopsy and the results showed some deterioration in certain areas of her liver. There was no improvement; her liver was still scarred and inflamed, and her out-patient consultant was struggling to control the other symptoms relating to her illness. Our time in the hospital was very worrying, and at times, we felt we were not being taken seriously about how ill she was.

After waiting for what seemed like a long time, the hospital consultants finally managed to see us and introduced themselves. This was like a dream come true for Tamara, as she thought they would prescribe some medication for the symptoms she was experiencing. However, she was left very disappointed by one of their remarks: "Tamara, you'll be going home and there is no reason why you shouldn't be in school." I could not believe the casual approach they were taking towards my daughter's ordeal, and I was left in a daze as to how real some of those people were.

Their comments astonished me, as they did not seek to find out how Tamara was feeling. Instead, they assumed that she was well. As if that wasn't enough, the next comment left me speechless: "Why are you in bed? You should be up and moving around. According to the biopsy, there are no significant changes to your liver, therefore there's no reason why you should not be in school."

Tamara and I both looked at each other in disbelief. There was pain and anguish in her eyes as she tried to make sense of what she had just heard. How on earth did they arrive at such conclusion when Tamara's medical notes clearly showed that she was suffering from many different complications, and was not able to regularly attend school? It appeared to me that they were not interested in Tamara's health.

How does school fit into the picture when this child is crying for death and is hardly able to cope with the hell she was going through? As a mother, I wanted the best for my child, just like any other responsible parent, but basic common sense told me that this child was clearly dying. Her inability to go out, frequent tummy pain, painful muscle spasms, voices in her head, vomiting and severe itching were only a few of the symptoms that she was experiencing. Tamara would be the happiest child to attend school because she liked school and would do almost anything to fit in with her friends. She felt lonely and abandoned as she was losing all her friends due to the illness. Wasn't that enough trauma for one child?

Tamara had been having private tuition for most of her life. She went to dance school and had piano lessons weekly. She also had private lessons in Mathematics, English and Science. All the extra tuition was to stop Tamara falling behind in her lessons, therefore the real problem wasn't about school, it was about giving her an opportunity to live.

As soon as they left the room, Tamara put her arms around me in despondency and said, "Mom, I know the doctors don't believe me, but I feel like I am going to die." How could a caring profession drive a twelve-year-old girl to such depths of despair? Her suffering would have been alleviated if there had been communication between the consultant and the parent. All that was necessary were a few questions to Tamara to find out how she was feeling. At the time when Tamara desperately needed the help and support, she was callously pushed to her lowest depths. To draw a conclusion based on a biopsy alone, without speaking to the parent or the child, is not only unwise but also unprofessional.

As a parent who watched her daughter's daily struggle for survival, I was left feeling numb with disappointment. Their remarks made me feel that my opinions as a parent did not matter, and Tamara's needs weren't a priority. Whether it was intended that way, I am not sure. However, should any doctor read this book, let me encourage you to treat each person as an individual and with the respect they deserve. The views of both the parents and children are important and should be taken seriously, because he "who feels it surely knows it."

Tamara's illness was not a minor problem, as one of her major organs was badly inflamed and scarred. It is a rare and incurable disease that is still being researched. It is also life threatening and affects approximately one in a hundred thousand children. Tamara's illness was getting worse and her outpatient consultant was doing her best, yet struggling to bring the illness under control. She became anaemic, her magnesium level was low, her eyes were extremely jaundiced and she struggled to walk short distances. In the midst of all that was happening, we continued to trust God, knowing that He could turn all situations around.

Although we were at the biggest crossroad in our lives, our faith in God remained steadfast, and our prayers became even more consistent as we released Tamara into His care.

CHAPTER TWENTY-FOUR
Pushed to the Edge

Tamara was discharged from the hospital and we were left feeling worse than when we went in. Her health gradually got worse, and she was now experiencing pains in her chest. The consultant's statement didn't make things better, and not only was she suffering from her physical ailments, but from the trauma of not being taken seriously. She became even more withdrawn and refused to speak to anyone about how she felt. Sometimes she asked, "Why don't they believe me when I feel so bad?" I really can't explain how I feel, but all I know is that I don't want to live anymore. Mom, why didn't you just let me die in your womb, why did you allow me to be born? I just want to die, I don't feel I can bear this anymore."

She could hardly get out of bed. The muscle spasms had increased, and the pains became so vicious that they interrupted her sleep. She was now entering the depression zone, as every now and then she would burst out into piercing screams and could not be consoled. Anyone associated with Tamara would know that she very rarely cried, unless she was in severe pain—this was one of those times. As a mother, it was heartbreaking to watch my daughter suffer and listen to her screams of anguish.

Although she was hesitant to share her feelings with us, she was encouraged to talk to someone she could trust. This she did and spoke frequently to two of her aunties, sharing her desire to die to get rid of the severe pain she was experiencing, and trying to explain what she was going through. Whenever Tamara needed them, they were with her in minutes. Because of our experiences, we felt we were being "pushed to the edge," however, our belief in God remained steadfast.

Our house was always packed to capacity as our church members, friends and relatives offered assistance and support. Tamara talked to her relatives and friends freely about the incident that took place at the hospital, and shared how let down she felt. Her only consolation was that her doctors at the local surgery and her outpatient consultant at the hospital—whom she saw on a regular basis—believed her. This consultant showed great care and concern, and her commitment to Tamara's well-being was without question. Tamara is very appreciative for the positive input she has made to her life.

Before Tamara started attending secondary school, I felt it appropriate to explain Tamara's illness to her teachers. I informed them of her diagnosis and some of the complications that she had experienced in the past. I reassured them that Tamara was doing well as the illness was controlled by various medications.

For the first few months whilst at secondary school, Tamara's health was fine. However, as time went by, it began to take a turn for the worse. Her attendance became irregular as she began to experience various attacks of the illness on her body and mind. Not only was she suffering physically, but also emotionally. She was unresponsive at times, staring into space, and occasionally seemed very distant. Her sleep was disturbed by constant conversations. Whenever I inquired she would say, "Mom, I am seeing things that frighten me and sometimes I hear voices. It's not good, is it?"

This was extremely worrying for us, so I called my cousin and told her what was going on. She suggested this might be due to the high temperature that she was also experiencing. It was still very unsettling because, although Tamara had had very high temperatures in the past, she never showed any signs of unusual behavior. It took me weeks before I understood that this behavior was due to the toxin from her liver entering her brain, causing confusion.

Sometimes, Tamara could not recall the events of the night. It troubled my mind, as she was hearing these voices even more frequently. Out of concern, I shared her experiences with her consultant, who was very understanding, however, she was not sure what was causing the symptoms. My fear was that Tamara was rapidly deteriorating and, as parents, we were unable to help her.

With all this stress and the enormity of our problem, we asked God to look after Tamara. She had lost her will to live and was slowly losing her fight for life. Our relationship had always been great, and she was her father's pride and joy. Our family life was beautiful and there was constant laughter in our home. Thank God, we have been blessed with a wonderful husband and a caring father. Although Tamara was a quiet child, at home she was the life and soul of the party, full of fun and mischief. All that was taken away from us and we were left empty and bewildered. We were faced with yet another overwhelming experience that was difficult to endure.

That night, I felt so overwhelmed that my husband had to console me as I sank into his arms and sobbed my heart out for our precious child. "I want my baby back, I want my Tamara back," I cried. How I wished that we could play Scrabble again and enter the singing contest that she used to arrange for our family. Grief overcame us and we felt physically weak and drained as we faced our challenges. In the daytime, she seemed much brighter, but she spent most of the nights awake due to various complaints. We regularly prayed to the God of comfort, handing over our child into His loving care. He was the only One we could rely on to maintain our sanity and surround our child with His hands of protection.

Tamara had an appointment for the following day to see an orthotist concerning her painful feet and joints. She was in terrible discomfort with pains all over her body and her main worry was, that she might end up in a wheel chair because of what was happening to her. The orthotist was a lovely man who was jovial and friendly. After putting Tamara at ease, he examined her feet and was shocked to see how flat they were.

Tamara explained how painful and difficult it was for her to walk short distances, and he was very understanding and sympathetic. He reassured her that he understood how painful the condition is, but it was not related to the liver problem. He immediately suggested ways of treatment and referred her to the physiotherapist for further assistance. On top of all that Tamara was going through, she was now faced with another nightmare. "When was this all going to end?" I thought. There seemed to be no end to her trauma.

We arrived home with a sense of relief, knowing that at least something would be done to alleviate her painful feet, but our burden was still overwhelming. We were exhausted and I felt a great sense of pity for our daughter. As I entered my front door, I felt as though my heart was broken in many pieces. My eyes caught a glimpse of the letters on the table and I picked up the first one, to discover that it was a letter from the Education Welfare Department. Part of the letter read:

Dear Mrs. Francis,

Your child has been referred to the Education Welfare Department due to her irregular attendance at school. Etc

Needless to say, I was devastated and angry at the same time. About three weeks earlier, during one of her routine appointments, I explained to Tamara's consultant about the hell she was going through. Out of sheer desperation and a sense of decency, I asked her to write a letter to Tamara's school, explaining that her absence was due to her illness, and not out of negligence. I had always kept the school fully informed about Tamara's progress and every visit to the hospital was explained to them. Tamara's consultant kindly wrote the letter, which I personally hand-delivered to her school. As a parent, there was nothing more that I could possibly do.

How could I then have received such a letter? How could someone be so cruel? Who could have called the Education Welfare Service after the nightmare that this young child was going through? I was barely able to cope with my daughter's ongoing problems, let alone something else. I fell to my knees in my living room and asked God—who sees and understands all things—for extra strength to cope with what seemed like an unbearable cross.

Out of sheer exhaustion and intense pain, I asked God, who had always been there for us, for help. I felt broken as the tears ran freely down my face. My eyes were now swollen from crying and my blouse was wet with tears. After what seemed like a long time on my knees, I

148

finally stopped crying. In that short space of time, I began to feel a strange peace as this scripture encouraged me: "God's grace is sufficient for you, and His strength is made perfect in your weakness for when you are weak, you are strong."

I immediately dried my tears, got up from my knees and joined the other members of my family in the dining room. I felt a sense of courage and, for that minute, I knew that I had a new challenge to face, but I was not alone. God was there with me and He was going to bring me through that nightmare, as He had done so many times before. I was, however, taken aback by the indiscretion and insensitivity of receiving such a letter at this time. How could such an error of judgment be meted out to someone already under so much pressure? This treatment was not only unfair, but also unnecessary.

On top of all that we were already experiencing we could well do without any more problems! However, with these thoughts in my mind, I was determined to vigorously challenge the injustice against our family. In my greatest hour of despair, I asked God for strength to deal with this extra burden.

I then called the school and spoke to Tamara's teacher, briefly explaining the contents of the letter. An appointment was made and I arrived at the school two days later. The teacher was lovely and showed a great sense of care and compassion. She made it very clear that the school was not responsible for informing the Education Welfare Department about Tamara's absence, as they were aware that Tamara was not well. She said it was obvious that she was clearly unwell by just looking at her. At that point, I didn't really care who believed me or not. All I knew was that my only daughter was dying, and somebody was gambling with her precious life.

A few weeks earlier the school was informed about the deterioration in Tamara's health and how she was struggling with the illness. The letter clearly stated that her absence from school was due to this problem. No one needed a medical book to see that something was seriously wrong with this child. Ordinary people on the street frequently stopped us, suggesting that Tamara be rushed to the hospital because of her appearance. "Was I missing something or was there something else happening that I wasn't aware of?" I asked myself over and over again. After I left the school, I made further inquiries as to the origin of the letter, and was sad to find out that certain individuals from the hospital were behind this sorry affair.

I was shocked to the bone that someone in a caring capacity could be so heartless. All my earlier fears were now becoming a reality. Most of the doctors at the hospital had always been brilliant, but I was beginning to realize that not everyone had my daughter's best interests at heart. It appeared that Tamara was just another statistic, another number on their list, who did not really matter to those involved. We were now left to ponder the reasons behind all of this. Tamara and I felt let down, due to this unfortunate experience, but we were determined to challenge this injustice against us.

Although we were faced with so many obstacles, I made it a priority to write a letter of complaint and sent letters to those involved, expressing our disgust at the unnecessary stress that we had been subjected to because of their unprofessional conduct. Everyone who had heard about the incident was left in shock, with a lot of questions. No one could believe that this was possible from anyone, let alone someone working in a caring profession.

Tamara's illness alone spoke for itself; her regular attendance at school prior to her recent problems and her inability to even go short distances was clear evidence this child was in serious trouble. Over the next few weeks, I had frequent communications with two of the consultants who tried to deal with the situation as best as they could. Life has taught me that it doesn't cost anything to show a little love and concern to our fellowmen, as one day, we will need the same from someone else.

CHAPTER TWENTY-FIVE
A Wilderness Experience

We found it difficult to come to terms with the unnecessary burden that had been forced upon us, but sincere love for our daughter and a determination to see her survive, urged us on. On top of all that we were going through, this was the last thing we were expecting to happen. Over the years, I had met various doctors concerning Tamara's illness, and they were supportive. The team always treated us with respect, and there was a sense that everyone was looking out for my child's best interest. Now, I felt very disappointed with the whole incident regarding the letter.

I realize that with all the medical knowledge a doctor may have, they will never fully understand the pain the sufferer goes through, unless they have been there themselves. I have the greatest admiration for the medical profession and deeply appreciate the work that they do, but the real heroes are the children who have had to battle with life-threatening illnesses day after day, yet still manage to smile. I have great respect for caregivers who dedicate their love and time to their loved ones without asking for anything in return. They are the ones who really know what happens when the night falls.

Tamara was still deteriorating, the pains had increased, the muscle spasms got worse, and she was physically and mentally exhausted. Her fingers and toes were stiffening more frequently, the itching had increased, her eyes were now bright yellow and her complexion had become incredibly dark. It was frightening to watch the changes in her body. She was now struggling to get out of bed and at times, had to be helped around. Our visits to the local doctor and the Emergency Department were frequent, as our twelve-year-old was obviously getting worse.

I was determined that my child would be treated fairly and with the dignity she deserved. I knew God was in control of the whole situation. He was the one looking after Tamara, even when some of the medications failed to work. With all the doom and gloom, I was aware that God had a plan for my daughter, and I constantly reminded myself of the vision God revealed to me when she was only a young child.

As our daughter grew weaker and weaker, we began to search for new solutions. We often watched various ministers on Christian TV who shared their testimonies of how they overcame tragedies. This gave us encouragement and strength to carry on. At times, we received prayers over the phone, other times we received letters of encouragement. Members of our church frequently visited to pray for the family.

On one occasion, a group of us went to a crusade. We took Tamara, in the hope that she would at least be encouraged. She sat down for most of the service due to the pain she was experiencing. The service was very inspiring and many people went to the front to be prayed for. As I listened to the songs and the scriptures, I prayed silently that God would bring some sort of relief to my daughter.

We had a wonderful time that night and, after the meeting, I greeted the minister, and expressed my gratitude for the powerful word he preached. As I approached him, he paused and asked, "Whose child is this?" I told him Tamara was my daughter, and he began to prophesy over her life. He said she was a very special child called by God, who was going to use her in a powerful way. He encouraged me to train her up to love the Lord. With these words, he looked on Tamara and said, "This child shall live and not die, to declare the works of God." I cannot remember if I had a chance to tell him about Tamara's illness, but I was grateful for the words of encouragement.

The following night, we went back to the meeting, and it was just as inspiring. Tamara appeared livelier than normal, and this time she was determined to enjoy the service. She desperately wanted to be well and was willing to try anything that would bring her relief.

The minister was a young man who was visiting from Uganda. He preached with much fervor and enthusiasm as he shared his experience about the love of God. The message was coming from someone who knew what suffering was all about. In his most difficult moments, his only source of comfort had always been his confidence in God. He was a victim of oppression, yet his faith in God was unwavering. I found great comfort from his testimony as I could relate to some of the things he shared. It was an uplifting time and, as I usually do at the end of the meeting, I greeted and encouraged him to continue ministering the Word.

After I shook his hand, he paused and asked whose child Tamara was. I told him that she was my daughter, and he began to prophesy over her life. He said he saw her preaching to hundreds of people and she was a very special child selected by God. To our utter amazement, this young man repeated the same words the minister spoke at the previous crusade: "This child shall live and not die, to declare the works of God." All my friends heard the revelation and they rejoiced with me. God was faithful to us and again reassured us that He was very present with us in our struggles. Thank God for the revelation, which brought us much hope and a renewed peace in our hearts and minds.

Over the next few weeks Tamara's health further deteriorated. In fact, she was steadily getting worse and the attacks on her body were even more furious. We continued to make numerous phone calls asking for prayers for Tamara. We were getting increasingly desperate as we listened to her frantic cries for help.

A feeling of helplessness overwhelmed me as I watched my daughter suffer, without being able to do anything about it. I called both my local doctor and the National Health Service helpline for advice. They were helpful and understanding, and it was heart-warming to know that there was someone I could talk to.

Some of the symptoms were new and, needless to say, very frightening for both Tamara and us. She was extremely fearful of the muscle spasms, which twisted her muscles out of shape, causing great distress and making it almost impossible for her to move.

After attending one of her appointments at the physiotherapist, Tamara decided that she would try to attend school. Her temperature was high and it was obvious that she was in great discomfort, yet she struggled her way to school. However, during the course of the day, Tamara felt worse and had to be collected and brought home.

By the time she got home, she was vomiting and unable to climb the stairs. My husband and I lifted her to her room and offered tablets to alleviate the pains. The following day she was back at her local doctor and was bedridden for most of the week.

During Tamara's illness, she spent many days praying that God would help her to cope with the pain and discomfort she was experiencing. She struggled to come to terms with the changes in her appearance and the constant barrage of ailments that were attacking her body, yet she still managed to encourage us when we felt weak. Prayer became a source of strength for our family, as everything else seemed to fail. Many of our relatives and friends prayed for strength in our times of weakness and God had always been faithful to us. We were often reminded to cast all our cares upon Him because He cares for us.

CHAPTER TWENTY-SIX
The Valley of the Shadow of Death

The incidents relating to Tamara's attendance at school were still fresh in my mind. It seemed as though everything was against us at the most vulnerable time in our lives, but I was determined to fight for my child's life. The trauma seemed unending, as we watched our daughter endure tremendous pain and suffering. Life seemed to have come to a standstill, and we felt as though we were traveling through "the valley of the shadow of death".

God remained faithful every step of the way, and I'm grateful for His unfailing love. The support from my church was overwhelming, as everyone rallied around to offer help. How wonderful it is to touch people's lives in a very positive way as we pass through this life. Any act of kindness is never forgotten.

A few weeks later, Tamara's fingers and toes began to stiffen involuntarily, and she had a hard time straightening them out. Everyone was in a state of panic as we watched our daughter suffering from an illness that we knew little about. Merrick and I helped as much as possible, but we were scared, as we were not sure what was going to happen next. The muscle spasms occurred more frequently and Tamara became even more petrified. She spent many days asking God to rid her of the discomfort, which was becoming unbearable.

A few days later, the stiffening of Tamara's fingers and toes returned. She also began to experience pains in her arms and legs. At this point, the pain had become so intense that she was almost unable to move. She wanted to go to her bedroom to rest, but her body wouldn't allow her. All of a sudden, a muscle spasm appeared in the back of her calf, and for the first time we were facing something that we'd never seen before. Her calf had become hard and rigid and became like a hard ball, which moved to the side of her leg.

By this time, Tamara was screaming at the top of her voice from the intensity of the pain. She was crying out, "Somebody please help me, please Mum, please Dad, help me, it's hurting so badly." Merrick and I massaged her leg as much as possible and, after what seemed like about five minutes of sheer hell, the pains slowly subsided. By now, Tamara was unable to walk. My husband and I lifted her upstairs and prepared her for bed.

When she reached the bedroom, a most vicious muscle spasm attacked her again. There was sheer panic on her young, tearstained face as she looked to us for reassurance. What could we do to help our daughter? We were weary of calling the hospital for advice, but Tamara kept screaming as the spasms got worse. The back of her calf had hardened so much until everyone became scared. Out of sheer desperation, and in a heightened state of panic, I called the emergency services. A lady answered my call, and in the background, she could hear Tamara's screams. I explained as best I could what was happening to my daughter, and she assured me they would send an ambulance as quickly as possible. The ambulance came within minutes; however, by the time they reached the house the muscle spasms had calmed down. I explained what had happened to Tamara and—fearing that the same episode would take place again—we took her to the emergency department. Tamara was so shaken by her experience that it left her dazed and panic-stricken. As usual, after her terrifying ordeal, she was hardly able to walk due to the effects of the muscle spasms in her legs.

The ambulance men were very caring, and they treated Tamara with respect. We arrived at the emergency department and Tamara had to be wheeled into the hospital. After what seemed like hours, a young doctor finally saw us. I explained what had happened to Tamara and was hoping for some solution to the problems.

He checked Tamara and, after all I had told him, he informed me that this was not an emergency case. I was shocked to the core to hear this doctor trivializing my daughter's experience. She was still sitting in the chair and unable to move properly, yet the doctor refused to take her situation seriously. Again, another person from the medical profession had knocked our confidence. A simple answer like "I'm not sure" or "I don't know" would have been more helpful than his total dismissal of her painful ordeal.

I may never know what effect his remarks had on Tamara, but her only comment was, "Maybe it would be better if I were dead, because nobody believes that I am dying anyway." She then turned her tearstained face to me and said, "Mom, are you sure he was a doctor?" I looked at her and said, "To be honest, my child, I'm not sure he is, but if he is, he should not be allowed to work with children."

Tamara would not accommodate any other comments about her experience. Her pains and disappointments were too deep to express. This insensitive doctor callously drove her into despair. In spite of all this, we never gave up hope, as we knew that God would never let us down or disappoint us, unlike our fellow humankind.

CHAPTER TWENTY-SEVEN
The Grim Reality of Liver Transplantation

On July 4, 2003, Tamara was again taken to casualty because of the muscle spasms. By now, her condition had worsened, she was hearing more voices, and at times seemed a little confused. Her eyes were bright yellow and her face had become swollen. Her once-pink lips were darker than before, her tummy was large and distended, and her hair was falling out from the progression of the liver disease. The itching had become more severe to the point of continuous sleepless nights, and it was painful to watch her suffering in this way.

This time, we arrived at the hospital to more friendlier and caring doctors. Everyone was brilliant. They carried out the tests, each time explaining the various procedures they were undertaking. At the end of the tests, we were told Tamara was very sick and had to be admitted immediately.

She was taken to Ward 8 where her care began. The nurses were kind and caring, and the parents of the sick children on the ward were very encouraging and supportive. All the children had their own stories about endurance, determination and their fight to survive against the odds.

One particular nurse had an uncaring attitude towards Tamara. Family members and friends often remarked about her lousy care and lack of understanding about the illness. There were times when the nurse stormed into Tamara's room, demanding that she got out of bed. Although she was barely able to move, the nurse accused her of being lazy. Instead of Tamara receiving the care she so much needed, the nurse's attitude caused more distress. Because of this, Tamara was hesitant to receive any further care from her.

The nurse's attitude only changed when I firmly told her that if the maltreatment continued, I would have no alternative but to write a formal letter of complaint against her. With many tears and apologies, she relented, and from then on Tamara was treated with the respect that she deserved. She later apologized to Tamara for her bad treatment towards her. How unnecessary this all seemed to be, when a little love and care was all that was expected from her.

Tamara's health rapidly deteriorated in the hospital. She was given a large cocktail of medication to try to combat the illness. It was obvious that she was having acute liver failure. The disease had progressed significantly and she was experiencing constant tummy pains, and at times she became irritable and confused. The heartache of watching our daughter go through the pangs of hell could not be put into words. Our only source of consolation was the fact that God was present with us in our struggles, and in His own time, He would make all things beautiful. All we could do was carefully place our daughter in His hands.

As I locked myself away in the hospital toilet, my tears flowed freely as I recalled the laughter, excitement and the wonderful times we shared together as a family. My words to God were few but meaningful as I asked Him for strength to cope with this big task that faced me. I prayed "Dear God, thank you for the opportunity to share in Tamara's life. At present, my heart is overwhelmed with grief and I am not sure how to handle it. Watching my daughter in pain is breaking my heart, and although I desperately want her to live, if you choose to take her back to yourself, please don't let her suffer. All I ask is that you send your angels briskly to whisk her away from all the pain, heartache and disappointments in this life." With this simple prayer, I sobbed freely as I released my burdens to God who knows and understands.

Tamara's condition worsened and her rapid deterioration was of grave concern to the doctors and nurses. She was unable to sleep at nights because of the hourly barrage of medications and the continuous tummy pains. The days were restless from lack of sleep and the regular intake of medications. Blood tests were frequent, the diarrhea and vomiting were taking their toll on her body, and she was rapidly losing weight. She was hooked up to different machines and needed assistance with getting around. Tamara had a few days when she felt a little better, and she would make the most of them by trying to walk around.

Since Tamara's diagnosis eight years ago, this was the sickest she had ever been. She was becoming progressively worse in front of our very eyes. There was always an excellent support network around us from the hospital. Beacon Evangelical Church, where we are members, stood alongside us every step of the way. They fasted and prayed for Tamara, supported my husband at home, and visited us regularly at the hospital.

Their letters of encouragement, numerous phone calls and their physical presence helped us through the most difficult times of our lives.

After being at the hospital for a while, I decided to go home for a break to see how my husband was coping with the rest of the family, while my friends volunteered to stay with Tamara until I returned. As I was getting ready to leave, one of the nurses told me that Tamara's consultant wanted to see me, along with my husband. I knew Tamara was very sick, but the consultants had not yet explained the seriousness of her condition.

My husband was unable to attend, as we were still fostering and he had the other children to deal with. He was doing an incredible job at home, and is the best husband anyone can have.

Tamara's consultant arrived, and I wasn't flustered or extremely nervous. She sat down in Tamara's room and discussed the seriousness of my daughter's condition. "Tamara is critical and there is nothing more anyone could do for her liver, as it is beyond treatment. Her only option is to have a liver transplant. Without this, she would not live to see her thirteenth birthday."

Although I knew that Tamara was very ill, I was not prepared to hear those chilling words. I was surprised to hear that my only daughter had just a few months to live, and there was nothing else they could do. "It's left to the one upstairs," she said. That man upstairs was God, who had been so close to us through our ordeal, and I was confident that He wasn't about to leave us now. The consultant explained that Tamara would be placed on the transplant list, where she would have a chance of receiving a liver. There was a waiting period of about three months, however, a liver could become available at any given time during that period. That was my daughter's only hope of survival.

Nothing prepared me for that moment as the tears ran down my face. My thoughts flowed freely as I tried to make sense of what the consultant had just said. I struggled to come to terms with liver transplantation, as I always had great difficulty with the mere concept of it. Very quickly, I calculated the months to her next birthday, which made eight months. "Eight months to live," I cried. "Oh, my baby, my baby, my only baby, oh God, please help me," I sobbed.

That day, I felt empty and broken and my heart felt like a shattered mess. Everything seemed senseless, and I wept for the most treasured gift God had given me. The doctor was patient, as I struggled to gain some composure. Shortly afterwards, the door slowly opened to the beautiful face of my wonderful niece, Sandra, who had always been there for us in our time of difficulty. She walked in to the whiff of hysteria and bathed me with comfort and reassurance. As her firm arms wrapped me like a blanket, it reminded me of God's sovereign love towards me.

After what seemed like hours, the doctor left the room leaving my niece and me. We talked for a long time until she was ready to return to work. I sat on my own for a while and marveled at how timely her appearance had been. She came at the time when I needed her most, and she certainly made a difference. As I thought about my daughter, I was revisited by the vision I had when Tamara was only two years old. The words from the vision ran through my mind: "Tamara will be sick to the point of death, but she shall not die but live." I was now more certain than ever that Tamara would live to declare God's praise. She was a special child who had a special purpose to fulfill.

Tamara had now returned from some activities with her play specialist, a remarkable and caring young lady. I looked at Tamara and remembered what the doctor had told me about her condition. I was overwhelmed with a strange kind of peace that reassured me that everything was going to be all right, although the intensity of my pain was beyond explanation. I wasn't sure how Tamara was going to be healed, but all I knew was that, in the end, she would be fine.

Over the next few days, many different individuals from the transplant team visited me, explaining in detail every step of the transplant procedures. I was given an information packet to read and shown the equipment in intensive care. Everyone in the team was brilliant, as they shared the positive aspects of liver transplantation and also the risk factors. My head was almost spinning from the information given to me. It was so much to take in, and this left me feeling that I was facing the biggest Goliath of my life. Their expertise and simple humanity impressed me and again gave me faith in the medical profession.

I really felt cared for and supported by the entire medical team. Everyone was aware that my daughter was seriously ill and their love and commitment willed us to carry on. After I signed the consent forms, Tamara was put on the transplant list. I was now left with no alternative but to give this enormous burden to God, who had so faithfully looked after our family in the past. It now became too much for me to bear, and I felt like I was approaching breaking point. Again, I wept and asked God for his strength in my weakness.

All the procedures were also explained to Tamara and this left me concerned about her emotional state. She was quiet as she absorbed the information and asked many questions. She was also nervous and frightened, and struggled with the concept of liver transplantation. The thought of someone dying, in order for her to live, was too much for her small mind to comprehend.

CHAPTER TWENTY-EIGHT
At Breaking Point

After a few days, Tamara's condition steadily grew worse. She was now hardly able to move and almost unresponsive. At times, she stared into space and was very confused. Extracting blood from her became difficult, therefore a neckline was inserted to do blood tests and give blood supplement. She was hooked up to different machines, with needles in both hands. Her blood sugar level was often low and she had high blood pressure. It was very clear that her health was swiftly going downhill. Joan, my sister, never gave up hope as she frequently read the scriptures to her and prayed for her. Again, I prayed to God, the restorer of broken lives, for help for my daughter. I asked Him for strength and courage to face what lay ahead as I felt weak and faint.

Although deep down, I knew that God would heal my daughter, it didn't take the pains away. Whenever I saw her in distress, my heart ached so badly, often reducing me to tears. There were times when I couldn't pray, but the church was praying for me. My nephew Craig was always there, helping the family and willing Tamara to carry on. People from many different countries also prayed for her recovery. We felt very supported during this difficult time.

The encouragement was heart-warming from families, friends and my wonderful church, Beacon. Our elders, Eric Jones and Timothy Turner—two of the very best leaders I have come across—stood alongside us and lavished God's love on us at the most vulnerable times of our lives. Oh, how God longs for people such as these who will stand in the gap for Him. I have nothing but appreciation and admiration for Beacon Evangelical Church, the very church in which I hold a leadership position, and one that I am proud to be a part of.

Tamara was now extremely thin, as she hadn't eaten for days. The constant vomiting and the lack of food had taken their toll on her body. She was so thin that she was hardly recognizable. Her face and eyes had lost their lust for life, and her ability to communicate sensibly was now being disrupted by voices in her head. Slowly we were becoming alienated from each other, like a man sojourning a dangerous battlefield with the prospect of death awaiting him. I longed to have an intelligent conversation with her, as we had so frequently done before. The rumbling voices of torment, and the void stare of detachment, had spookily enchanted my world and left me in a state of horror and bewilderment.

The doctors and nurses kept a close eye on Tamara and were painfully aware of her deteriorating condition. I knew she had gotten worse, but I did not know the medical term for her present prognosis. Later that day, upon the advice of the doctors, she was moved to the high dependency unit, where she had one nurse in charge of her care. Basic common sense told me that Tamara's health was spiraling out of control, and something was seriously wrong.

My friend, Sonia Lawrence and my three other cousins were visiting when I was told that the doctors wanted to see me. I reluctantly left Tamara in the capable hands of the nurses, who had cared so well for her. Sonia had been a tower of strength to us. She devoted all of her holiday to help in the care of her goddaughter. There was hardly a day when she wasn't at Tamara's bedside, encouraging her and supporting us in our struggles. Thank God for the many people who gave us hope to carry on.

I went with the doctors to the other side of the hospital, where we all sat down. I was confronted with yet more heartbreaking news about my daughter. This time, I was told that she was in a semi-coma and had only a few weeks to live. The toxin from the liver had now entered her brain and left her in a state of confusion. I was told that the only one thing left for them to try was a liver dialysis. This was a process of extracting all the blood from her body and purifying it in order to remove some of the toxin from her brain. The doctors weren't sure if it would work, but this would buy her some time as she waited for a new liver.

There were also varicose veins and ulcers in her stomach that were bleeding profusely. A minor operation was needed to place small rubber bands around the veins in order to reduce or stop the bleeding. Everything was moving very fast and Tamara was now in a critical state. The need for a liver was even more desperate than ever as my daughter was drifting away from us very swiftly.

Tamara had been placed on the liver transplant list and the waiting continued. In the meantime, all the tests were carried out to prepare her for the biggest ordeal of her life. She had been given the operation to tie the varicose veins in her stomach, and was later rushed down to the intensive care unit to have the liver dialysis. She was in a state of confusion as the toxin was affecting her brain. She was no longer aware of my presence, as she drifted in and out of consciousness.

As the necessary preparations were made for Tamara's liver dialysis, I walked over and laid my hands on her. Again, I gave her to the God of mercy and love and asked Him to look after her. I prayed, "Dear God, when we were desperate for a baby, we prayed and asked for a child that we would love and appreciate, and you gave us Tamara. This is the same baby that we have suckled and loved all her life, but here she is now, at the point of death, and suffering beyond belief. There is nothing more we can do but hand her faithfully back into your care for you to look after."

By this time, my face was drenched with tears and my eyes were swollen and puffy from crying. Again, I lost my composure as I quietly and painfully released my only child into God's care. I prayed for the doctors, nurses, and for every sick child and their parents who were in the same position as myself.

Later that day, Tamara was hooked up to the dialysis machine and another ordeal began. As the liver dialysis began, Tamara started to show slight improvement. She was slowly gaining some sort of consciousness and was now beginning to make sense again. The process was slow but it was definitely making a difference. We were now able to have intelligent conversations and once more, we saw the Tamara we had lost, slowly coming back. Her friend Selina laughed and joked with her.

Everyone was ecstatic to see the improvement. At times, she was in obvious discomfort, as she found it difficult to lie in a comfortable position, but she managed to cope.

It was almost unbearable to see other sick children suffering in intensive care, let alone our own child. The doctors and nurses were brilliant, and they showed commitment and dedication in the care of my daughter. She was given numerous medications, had regular blood tests, and was losing weight rapidly. There were still times when she drifted in and out of consciousness, but it was apparent she was determined to fight for her survival.

Everyone was praying for Tamara. The nurses, who had grown to love her, visited her frequently, and the parents, who were struggling with their own children, willed us on with their wonderful encouragement. Family members and friends from different countries called to support us in our struggles, and the local radio station announced her illness and encouraged listeners to pray.

Sandra, my niece, and Sonia had always been at Tamara's bedside. They had committed themselves to be there at this very crucial time for our family. I would not have coped without their help, as I was both mentally and physically drained. Overwhelming exhaustion and tremendous pain were taking a firm grip on my body and mind. I was now beginning to buckle under the pressure as I wept continuously for my daughter. It was getting all too much for me to bear, as I watched Tamara's frail body being attached to drips, needles and different machines. Very often, when I found it too difficult to cope, Sonia and Sandra were there; ready to take over the care of my daughter.

Tamara's liver dialysis for the day was now completed. It was incredible to see how quickly she reverted to the same state of confusion that she was in before the liver dialysis. She was again entering the "semi-coma zone." I wept bitterly because I was no longer able to communicate with her.

Just when I thought I couldn't take any more, Tamara began vomiting huge amounts of blood. We stood in a state of helplessness, and everyone seemed dumb with disbelief. I asked myself, "Is this really happening? Could this be a very bad dream that I would eventually wake from?" How I wished it were a dream from which I would wake up in a minute, and this sorry affair would be over.

To my greatest horror, the brutal reality dawned on me that there was a strong possibility my daughter may die that night, and I collapsed into sheer panic. From my inner being, I muttered something to God that went like this, "I know that you are still with us, but why don't you do something and do it now?" I then composed myself and encouraged Tamara, telling her everything would be all right. I told her I had given the whole situation to God and He would look after her. She nodded her head in agreement.

CHAPTER TWENTY-NINE
A Glimmer of Hope

Sandra and Sonia encouraged Tamara, and supported her in every way possible, sometimes praying for her, and other times holding her hands and willing her on to live. My husband was doing a tremendous job at home looking after the other three children, two in foster placement and my nephew, who had lived with us since he was a baby. Despite being under a lot of pressure, he still managed to make frequent visits to the hospital.

Later that day, I approached the threshold of despondency, as I held my daughter's frail hands and watched her drift in and out of consciousness. It was difficult to take my eyes off her, as I was afraid we would lose her. There was no alternative but to remind myself of the vision I had when she was only young, and I desperately tried to console myself with the words that the two preachers had given me, "Tamara shall not die but live to declare the works of God."

I found myself climbing higher and higher into the arms of despair, and for a while, I felt frozen with fear and trepidation, intimidated by the very thought of death. My own fear was strangling me like a rope gripped tightly around an animal's neck, which had mercilessly left it gasping for precious air. Such was the massive overdose of pain that had been inherited from our ordeal that I felt exposed to icy shivers of agitation and discouragement. Somehow, the insurmountable grief was blinding my vision and my faith in God's ability to preserve my only child's life was ebbing away.

The cruelty of death was too real for me, and I found myself wrestling with my faith. Marred by anguish and distress, I relentlessly tried to will myself to peer through the pitch darkness of my doubts and recapture my faith in God, who can turn all situations around. This I did with great struggle, as I studied two different scenarios I was confronted with. One was the reality of a dying child in intensive care with tubes all over her body; and the other was based on a simple faith in God, who would heal her. I was left to choose between the clear evidence of a dying daughter and my faith in God to deliver her. There was no choice but to believe in God, the restorer of broken things. I spoke the word of God repeatedly as the images of death stalked my mind.

By this time, Tamara had slowly drifted into semi-consciousness, and for a while, she looked peaceful. I used the opportunity to release the tears that had formed a huge lump in my chest, and I prayed for deliverance from my ghastly torment. How can anyone describe pain except through tears and lamentations? Here I was, buckled under the intense pressure that was almost pushing me over the edge.

At times, I felt as if I was crying my daughter's tears for her, as she was unable to express her pains. Broken and weak, I was callously driven on a lonely journey through the mud of despair. So dirty and filthy was I with grief, it was hard to see anything positive. The immense trauma had muddled up my vision, and the will to carry on was slowly waning. Left with no alternative, I awkwardly disclosed my misery to my friends: "I don't feel I can carry on for much longer, as I feel stretched to breaking point." I sobbed. Had I not expressed my pain, I would have overstepped the boundaries and approached the destructive road of insanity.

Out of the corner of my eye, I could see one of the doctors coming towards us. He was friendly and caring, and had previously treated Tamara. That wasn't a big deal to us, as doctors frequently visited the intensive care unit to check how their patients were doing. It was a relief to see him approaching Tamara's bedside, as I wanted to make sense of the enormous amount of blood she had vomited, and also her deteriorating condition. I was convinced he came because of the earlier incident, and to shed some light on her present condition.

As the doctor came closer, I proceeded to tell him about the huge amount of blood that Tamara had just vomited. However, he pleasantly interrupted me with a smile and asked cautiously, "Haven't you heard?" "Yes," I replied, "I was told that the doctors managed to reduce the bleeding from the varicose veins."

He looked at me, still smiling, and asked a second time, "Haven't you heard?" By this time, I was confused and asked," Heard what, doctor?" Filled with emotion and excitement, he said, "Mrs. Francis, a liver has been found for Tamara, and the liver transplant will take place early tomorrow." The news came like an unsuspecting tornado and nearly blew me off my feet. For a brief while, it was difficult to capture exactly what he was saying, but again I sensed a glimmer of hope.

Mercy and favor had found me in my greatest hour of despair. A liver had been found. Those words kept going around in my head and for a while, I couldn't move as I stared the doctor in the face. As the reality dawned on me, floods of tears, laughter, and loud moaning bellowed from my innermost being. I gripped the doctor with both hands, hugging him and almost lifting him off the floor through sheer expression of gratitude. Words could not describe my feelings of elation as the doctor freely celebrated with me.

My sunken eyelids were drenched with tears, as I expressed my thanks to the doctor and to God, for giving my daughter a second chance of life. Sonia, who was standing beside me, wept for joy at the good news. We held hands and wept aloud in the intensive care unit, almost forgetting where we were. Other parents quietly celebrated with us as they gave us the "thumbs up."

I wept for a good hour at the sound of the greatest news I had heard in a long time, but I was also in turmoil. The fact that somebody had to die for my daughter to live had undoubtedly left me dazed and confused. The reality of the whole situation startled me. "It wasn't just a liver, it was another person's organ or body part," I pondered to myself. The more I tried to make sense of it, the more confused I became. It was apparent that, somewhere out there, the parents of the organ donor were mourning their loss, while I was at the hospital celebrating and rejoicing.

Despite all the information given, nothing could prepare us for this moment. The feeling of guilt overwhelmed me, while at the same time I was gripped with a sense of elation, and I wasn't sure what or how to feel anymore.

With mixed emotion, I walked over to Tamara's bedside, praying that she would be able to understand what I was about to say to her. As I approached her bed, I excitedly called her name—Tamara—and to my

177

greatest surprise, she opened her eyes and looked at me. At this point, I could not contain my emotion as I told her that a liver had been found.

At the sound of those words, it appeared as if my frail daughter went into a state of shock, as she closed her eyes and refused to engage in any more conversation. After a few minutes, she opened her eyes and tearfully asked, "Haven't I had the liver transplant yet?" I answered carefully and gently, explaining that she had not yet had the transplant, but she would be fine. She then blurted out painfully, "What am I doing in intensive care if I haven't had the operation? Oh God," she cried, "I thought I had the liver transplant already. I am so scared," she said quietly as she drifted off into semi-consciousness. That was the last conversation we had before the transplant. For my thirteen-year-old, it was all too much to take in.

Before I left her bedside, all I could do was ask God to take care of her. I was too overwhelmed to engage in much conversation with anyone else, so I asked Sonia to call the church and as many people as possible to inform them of the news.

I called my husband and a few more people and told them of the developments, before retiring to the hospital room that was kindly given to me for a few weeks. Once I got there, I threw myself on the bed and wept bitterly. I found myself crying for the organ donor's parents and my daughter.

The last few months had taken their toll on me and I felt shattered, broken and confused. I spoke honestly to God and told Him how I was feeling. I also asked Him for help in clarifying the many unsolved questions that I had. I gave Him thanks for the family that donated the liver and thanked Him for the prospect of life for my daughter.

CHAPTER THIRTY
The Liver Transplantation

The day scheduled for the liver transplant was July 9, 2003. Doctors and nurses began making the necessary preparations for my daughter's liver transplantation. During the day, many people visited me from the medical profession, explaining their different roles and informing me of the complex procedure that would be undertaken. I signed many consent forms during the course of the day, and was pleasantly overwhelmed by many well-wishers who called, visited and encouraged us.

One by one, family and friends drifted in to support us. Different people brought supplies of food and drinks, and I was guaranteed at least one hot meal per day. People whose lives I had touched in one way or the other were now touching mine, and it was a very pleasant and heartwarming feeling.

I wasn't sure how much Tamara understood regarding the transplantation, as we weren't able to have any more conversations. She was very agitated and fought for a comfortable position in which to lie, tossing and turning all the time. She was already attached to a machine for the liver dialysis treatment, while others had been set up for her after-care. The sight of them was very frightening. By this time, I was a nervous wreck, all too aware of the enormity of the operation and the risks involved.

Again, fear tried to conquer me and I found myself sinking into the depths of despair. The magnitude of the risks involved sent spasms of anxiety through my body. Everything stood still for a while as my mind wearily wandered off to a place of "What if?" I could almost hear myself, as I filtered through the threads of negative imaginations, asking all the obvious but unnecessary questions. What if this is the last time I see my daughter? What if anything goes wrong? For a while, it seemed like I was kidnapped and held hostage by anxiety and fear. The feeling of despondency often visited me, and my heart felt as though I had been shot and wounded with many bullets. This was my only child.

With all the negative things happening in my mind, I was frequently interrupted by the overwhelming presence of a superior being who constantly reminded me of the visions I had in the past. Very clearly, I could hear the words the ministers told me about my daughter. Again, I became aware of my closest friend, God, reminding me that all would be well. Tearfully, I repented for trusting in my own feelings rather than in the power of God.

As soon as I released Tamara into God's care, He brought a peace upon me that was beyond explanation. That very minute, I knew my daughter would be fine. All that was left to do was to hand over to God all the doctors and nurses who were involved in Tamara's care. This I did, while at the same time, releasing all my cares unto the One who is touched with the feelings of our infirmities.

My steps were much brisker and lighter, as God gave me some relief from my cares. The idea of tubes down Tamara's nose and throat, neck lines, cannulas sticking out of her veins, and an incision in her tummy to extract the fluid, was of great concern to me, but God gave me a sense of calm. He also sent people to support me when I was weak and frail. My cousin, Tulla, had been a tremendous help supporting us in every way possible. She also helped to simplify some of the complicated medical language for us. Another cousin of mine, Shelia, came from London to offer encouragement.

After all the necessary preparation for the operation, my minister, friends and the majority of my church came to have prayers with us. They all prayed for Tamara and released her into God's care.

I stayed at Tamara's bedside for most of the night, giving God thanks for the beautiful child He had given me and asking Him to look after her. Tamara was not aware we were there, as she was in a state of semi-consciousness, and upon the advice of the nurses, I retired to bed. I was unable to sleep properly, as my daughter was at the forefront of my mind.

Approximately six o'clock the following morning, I was back at Tamara's bedside for the final preparations. At about eight o'clock, she was wheeled off to the operating theatre, accompanied by myself, Selina, my niece Sandra, along with the nurses and the transplant coordinator. At long last, there was a glimmer of hope for a little girl who was going to survive against all odds. The operation was due to last between six to eight hours.

The hours seemed to creep by as we waited in eager expectation for the results. Every few hours, the coordinator came and told us the progress of the operation. The news was always positive, and we took the opportunity to thank God for His mercies and faithfulness. We continuously prayed for guidance for the doctors and nurses, and thanked God for their skills.

Finally, the operation was over. We were greeted with the greatest news that we had heard in a long time. The liver transplantation was a success and Tamara was now, hopefully, on her way to recovery. There was great rejoicing everywhere as the news spread around. Nurses, doctors, and everyone who knew Tamara from the hospital, all rejoiced at one of the greatest miracles of all. The church celebrated with praise to the Almighty God for giving our precious daughter a second chance of life. They prayed for all those involved and thanked God for the skills He'd given to the surgeons.

She was back in the intensive care unit, hooked up to many different machines, with pieces of equipment attached to her. Our outlook on her life was now hopeful, as we were no longer bombarded with the frightening look of death; instead, we were embraced with abundant life and a much brighter future for our only child. God was fulfilling the vision He had given me when she was about two years old, and the ministers' prophecies were slowly coming to pass. We thanked God for honoring His word and showing us again that He can be trusted.

Tamara's condition improved steadily over the coming days, and she was soon out of intensive care. It was heartwarming to see her communicating with people and the old Tamara slowly returning. Soon she was in the high dependency unit, which was a clear sign that things were continuing to improve. She was given a large cocktail of drugs and her body was responding well to them.

Sometimes it is hard for us to fathom God and the strategies He used to work things out for His own good. For a child, it's even harder, especially when they are at their lowest. Although Tamara grew up in church and had learnt to pray and trust God at an early age, she reached a crossroad in her life, which undoubtedly shook her faith. During the most difficult period of her illness, she became disappointed with God as she felt that He wasn't capable of answering her prayers. In her situation, she prayed relentlessly for God to heal her and take away the pains, but the more she prayed, the more the pains got worse, and her condition became desperately critical. Because of this, she reached a point of unbelief and was losing faith in a God whom she wasn't sure existed anymore. Our prayers for her became a matter of urgency as we asked God that He would again make Himself known to her, to reaffirm her faith in Him.

About the third day after the operation, the nurse who was looking after Tamara greeted me. Her report was that Tamara was waving, smiling, and declaring that she had seen Jesus. According to the nurse, it appeared that she was hallucinating, so they lowered her morphine level. On the following night, my daughter awakened me from my sleep. Radiating with beauty and a peace that I had not seen for a long time, she pointed to the ceiling, smiling, and said, "Look Mum, look at the beautiful angels, they are flying all over my bed. How beautiful!" I explained to Tamara that I was unable to see them and she was shocked, but continued to admire these angelic beings for a few minutes, trying to describe them as they encircled her bed. I was delighted as I watched my daughter shine with delight and happiness.

The following day, Tamara was full of joy. She explained to me that she was not hallucinating as the nurses and doctor thought. She reassured me that she definitely saw Jesus smiling at her with His hands outstretched, and how the experience gave her much joy and comfort.

With this, she said, "Mom, I think I'll be a better Christian because of my encounter with Jesus." Tamara has been a changed person since the operation.

Today, Tamara is like any healthy teenage child, back at school and enjoying life again. It's now nearly three years since the liver transplantation, and I can hardly recognize my daughter. She is full of confidence and has a determination that cannot be easily swayed by anyone. She is doing well at school and is back in the swing of things. She shared her testimony with the church and other people that she came in contact with. As a deacon at Beacon Evangelical Church, I continue to share our testimony at every given opportunity, and will do so for the rest of my life. We are eternally grateful to God for giving us back our daughter.

As for our family, we cannot help but be grateful for our daughter's life, which was made possible through the death of someone's child. A million thanks to the parents who kindly donated their child's liver to my daughter. In closing this chapter of our lives, let me encourage every reader to CARRY A DONOR CARD, as life can be made possible through TRANSPLANTATION.

CHAPTER THIRTY-ONE
Rising from the Dust

Over the years, I have learnt that we are never alone through our hell and high waters experiences and that survival is possible with the help of God. It is through failures, hardships and pain that we often find strength, courage and determination to succeed against all the odds.

I have discovered that one of the most vital elements for survival in the midst of complexity is hope. It is like the hand that guides us through darkness and despair towards our destiny. On the contrary, accepting defeat in the midst of trauma is like the rope that binds us and kills our dreams. Therefore, for us to rise from the dust we must endeavor to become disassociated from a defeatist attitude. Our goals should be to strive to succeed even when the tide is against us, knowing that there is light at the end of the tunnel. There is always a way out.

The trauma of my childhood in Jamaica has had a devastating effect on my life, yet it has taught me very valuable principles from which I have grown and developed. Those experiences, however negative, have better equipped me with an avid determination to use my past as a stepping-stone for the future. They have also enabled me to deal with other setbacks I encountered, along with the ongoing battle of my daughter's illness. Many important lessons have been learnt and although it hasn't been easy, I am confident that God can use my experience to shape my destiny.

Whenever I had been tempted to run away or give up, God somehow gave me the courage to get up and move on. The real winners are those who refuse to quit and will dare to keep going rather than remain in the dust. It is therefore imperative for us to persevere even when all the odds are stacked against us, knowing that God is always present to see us through. With His help, we can rise up with wings like eagles and make steady leaps towards our goals.

In 2 Corinthians 4: 8-9 it says, "We are often troubled, but not crushed, sometimes in doubt but never in despair; there are many enemies, but we are never without a friend; and although badly hurt at times, we are not destroyed." This scripture assures us that whatever our circumstance, we can triumph over adversity and live an overcoming and victorious life. This process demands specific actions from those who are determined not to let their past dictate their destiny, but instead use their experience as a stepping stone to greater things. There is therefore no time to give up, for healing and restoration is available to those who are willing to release their past into the reliable hands of God.

The lessons learnt have been invaluable and have made me a better person. Not only has it helped to mould my character but it has also shaped my destiny. It is evident that God has used my experiences to equip me for a greater purpose in life. His commitment to see us through the obstacles should cause us to have an unwavering determination to rise above our circumstances.

Today I look back with a sense of gratitude for every step of my journey, for it is in pain that I experience God's divine healing. It is in those sad and lonely periods that I felt the warmth of His supernatural presence. As time goes by, the virtue of forgiveness has had greater significance during the times of ridicule and abuse. Each chapter of my life has been filled with good and bad times, yet they serve as a reminder of God's faithfulness and His ability to pick up the fallen and downtrodden of society.

The discovery of healing, restoration and forgiveness in the midst of suffering is an uplifting experience. I no longer look at my life with disgust and bitterness. Instead, I see it as a channel through which I can help others. The chains that bound me to sexual abuse have now been broken, and I have been enlightened by the fact that there is life after abuse. I have been blessed because of this knowledge, and I am grateful to God for helping me to embrace life with the assurance that whatever happens, God is more than able to bring me through.

My life is a work-in-progress, therefore my journey hasn't ended. There are yet many more mountains to climb, many obstacles to face and many battles to win; nevertheless, I am confident that God, in His infinite love and mercy, will continue to guide me as He has so faithfully done before. As I bring this chapter to a close, let me encourage you to have a determination not to lie down and die in the midst of trauma and heartbreak, but to rise from the dust with the help of God.

Postscript

Are You Ready To Change?

Are your past traumas and ordeals still enslaving you?
They will only enslave you if you allow them to. Take steps to try and move on. You'll discover that there is more ahead than what's left behind. Use your past as a stepping-stone to your destiny.

Are you still in bondage because of sexual abuse?
Seek help and get the necessary counseling. Don't let your abuse have the last say or it will keep you bound. Release the abuser through the power of forgiveness and you'll find that in time you will be able to move on. There is life after abuse.

Are you living in the past? Are your pains and disappointments keeping you there?
If so, recognize where you are and seek help in moving on. There is a greater future ahead of you.

Have you been ridiculed because of your appearance?
Look for the good in yourself and use it to empower other people. You'll find that you are more beautiful than how you look.

Are you blinded with anger and rage because of past hurts? Does your life revolve around revenge?
If so, find a different focus and use your energy in a more constructive way. Revenge will not only cripple you, it will destroy you and rob you of your future.

Today Let Your Motto Be:

I will not allow my circumstances to hold me captive. Nothing will stop me from fulfilling my destiny because my past does not dictate my future.

Don't let the dust settle - THERE IS ALWAYS A WAY OUT.

ABOUT THE AUTHOR

Almina Rose Francis was born 1959 in the district of Mount Industry, Jamaica. She is the sixth of nine children. Her life has borne witness to poverty and social deprivation.

At thirteen years old Almina suffered sexual abuse which shattered her world. She later became a Christian and attended her local Baptist Church.

Haunted by emotional abuse and facial disfigurement, Almina plunged into an ocean of despair. Nevertheless, she managed to bounce back with a tenacious determination to overcome the obstacles that faced her.

Almina's only daughter, Tamara, was diagnosed with a rare and incurable illness called Autoimmune Chronic Hepatitis. This resulted in liver failure and she was given only weeks to live. Watching the incredible suffering her daughter endured, Almina found herself faced with yet another traumatic ordeal. Despite all this, and the recent liver transplantation of her daughter, Almina learnt to rely completely on God.

Although it has been very difficult to revisit her past, Almina shares her moving and heartrending story of triumph over tragedy and hope against despair.

Almina lives with her husband, two foster children and her nephew, Keiron. She currently resides in Birmingham, England, is a deacon of Beacon Evangelical Church and has ministered in churches both in Jamaica and England. She studied Christian Education and worked as a teacher in Jamaica.

A book alone could not hold the many memories and experiences of the author's life story, but her account is a cocktail of sadness, humor and enduring strength.